Indian Family System

The Concept, Practices and Current Relevance

Indian Family System

The Concept, Practices and Current Relevance

Edited by

Bal Ram Singh

Center for Indic Studies
Dartmouth (USA)

D.K. Printworld (P) Ltd.
New Delhi (India)

Cataloging in Publication Data — DK
[Courtesy: D.K. Agencies (P) Ltd. <docinfo@dkagencies.com>]

Indian family system : the concept, practices and current relevance / edited by Bal Ram Singh.
p. cm.
Contributed articles.
Includes bibliographical references.
ISBN 13: 9788124605936

1. Families — India. 2. Joint familie — India. 3. Civilization, Hindu. I. Singh, Bal Ram, 1958-

DDC 306.850954 22

ISBN13: 978-81-246-0593-6 **ISBN10: 81-246-0593-9**
First published in India in 2011

Published by:
Center for Indic Studies
University of Massachusetts, Dartmouth
285, Old Westport Road
Dartmouth, MA - 02747 (USA)
Phone: 508-999 8588 *Fax*: 508 999-8451
Email: bsingh@umassd.edu *Website*: www.umassd.edu/indic

and

Published and printed by:
D.K. Printworld (P) Ltd.
Regd. Office: 'Vedaśrī', F-395, Sudarshan Park
Ramesh Nagar Metro Station, New Delhi-110 015-11
Phones: (011) 2545 3975; 2546 6019; *Fax*: (011) 2546 5926
E-mail: indology@dkprintworld.com, *Website*: www.dkprintworld.com

Printed by: D.K. Printworld (P) Ltd., New Delhi.

Preface

GROWING up in India during 1960s and 1970s, family was everything that one had. Every decision, from areas of studies, marriage, and job, was decided in accordance with the family consideration. Living in the United States for over two decades, most of Indian Americans try to learn philosophical underpinnings of their family traditions even as they encounter an alien culture and tradition on a daily basis. There are constant questions about their food, dress, family, religion, and other traditions. But the most dominating topic of discussion remains the arranged marriage system of India. There is so much curiosity and awe with such a system. However, their awkward questions and looks also reflect a degree of disdain for the system as well. Such situations beg for better and deeper basis of the traditions. This is especially becoming relevant as the Indian American families are the most stable group in the United States.

Personally, I grew up in a village as part of a joint family. Even though my father passed away about three months before I was born, I actually never realized that I did not have father until I was seven years old. My uncle, four generations apart from us, is still the head of the family amongst men. My mother remained the head of the family amongst women as long as she was alive (until 2004). As I travelled through towns, cities, metropolises, to the United States growing up through education and jobs, this part of my life kept raising more and more conflicts personally and philosophically. Many pros and cons have been presented by family and friends for my continuous support to my joint family in the village, visiting them every year, and, as much as possible, treating them the same as my nuclear family living with me in the United States. I have based my action on my own experience, and have tried to rationalize with the philosophy of the tradition. This has led me to reflections and introspections in view of the changing world where many of the value systems have changed, and are replaced with legal and new social norms.

Concepts of joint and extended families in India exist more as practices than prescriptions, and are largely visible in the rural India. The system in place in rural India is easier to understand, as people live in vicinity, follow similar lifestyle, have similar outlook of life, and have similar social and spiritual needs. My experience in rural India was in conflict with the experience I had in cities in India, and I always felt that given the constraints of limited resources, space, and freedom of lifestyle, the joint family system may not be applicable in the urban India. This was my conflict until I met Chandra Mohan Bhandari, who was joint secretary in the External Affairs Ministry of the Government of India in 2005, and had been ambassador to Cambodia and Consul-General to Canada. Subsequently, he became ambassador to United Arab Emirates and Poland. He had mentioned to me about his joint family existing at that time while he was obviously away from his ancestral home. That conversation I had with him in Delhi in 2005 in fact triggered the concept of organizing a symposium on Indian Family System, as I was inspired to bring out the idea of joint family system to the modern world, using Bhandari's family which mostly lived in cities taking up jobs in different cities. One of his brothers was a professor at IIT Kanpur, while another lived in the village. I believe another of his brothers lives in the United States. But somehow they have kept the basic concepts of a joint family running. He reflects his experiences and ideas in his chapter entitled "Joint Family System".

The Symposium on the Indian Family System opened my eyes to a lot of information previously unknown to me. As it happens in society frequently, certain institutions established with best intentions and substantial planning become stale and ritualistic over a long period of time. Philosophical underpinnings and social capitals of the systems get lost or at least taken for granted. The family system seems to have unfortunately reached that state, and a discussion must take place on the basic values which may have provided inspiration for such a system.

I am grateful to contributors who agreed with me on the necessity of a discussion on this topic, and who wholeheartedly supported the concept by joining at the symposium and for submitting their articles. The articles represent social, economic, business, scientific, and spiritual aspects of family traditions. It is hoped that there is sufficient coherence of the chapters for the reader to get an overview of the issues involved.

I am grateful to my assistant, Miss Shwetha Bhat, for helping me put together the proceedings. I would also like to thank my administrative assistant, Ms. Maureen Jennings for helping in organizing the Symposium. Dr. Sukalyan Sengupta's help along with his assistant, Mr. Kumar, is appreciated. I would also like to express my appreciation to Ms. Heather Tripp and Ms. D. Confar of UMass Dartmouth's Photographics Department.

Finally, financial support from the Center for Indic Studies and Education Society for the Heritage of India is gratefully acknowledged.

Bal Ram Singh

Contents

Introduction

Bal Ram Singh

The Evolutionary Concept of Family

FAMILY is not just an optimum number of people who live together, but is a foundation of the society anywhere in the world. However, such foundations are of humans, and thus subject to human frailties as much as to the devotion, dedication, perseverance, and patience. While there are innate traits in all of the creations in this world, humans have been rendered with the instrument of intellect, perhaps more than others, to construct their thoughts and make decisions accordingly. A culture is thus developed from these constructions and thoughtful actions. Variations in such cultures are natural as are the natural living conditions of geography and climatic habitat, biodiversity and sustenance over a long period of time, and development of diverse philosophical and social thoughts.

Survival and reproduction have been considered as hallmark of the evolution process. Current model of evolution generally considers this survival and reproduction to be a selfish trait which drives all organisms to compete, adapt, and advance. There is ample evidence for such evolutionary process based on a trail of fossil records, phenotypic complexities, and perceived notion of human superiority amongst all living beings. The latter notion appears to affirm the selfish behaviour of individuals, which eventually forms the basis of association a person makes in the society, including family and friends.

Evolution, being a modern scientific concept, provides much of the moral authority to individuals to work for selfish interest, be it inside or outside the family. Such behaviour has been detrimental to the ideas of joint and extended family systems practised in the Indian subcontinent for thousands of years. Additionally, the industrial revolution that dawned over the past two centuries or so has had significant impact on the societal shift, more towards nuclear and fragmented nuclear families in the modern world. To understand root causes of the family fragmentation one has to look into this philosophical shift in the world today, and corrective measures taken at that level will automatically result in behaviours of individuals amenable to more cohesive family.

To address the issue and role of selfishness and its influence in social as well as scientific parlance of today's world, one has to understand the origin of such a philosophy. Living in the United States for the past 27 years, I have personally seen much contrast between fundamental social issues of India (East) and the Western world. The Western world has increasingly controlled the intellectual discourse for much of the past half millennia, and has thus defined the paradigms of knowledge and norms. In my conversation with a philosophy professor at Jawaharlal Nehru University in India, Dr R.P. Singh, he tried to contrast the philosophy of East and West by defining the position of man in the world. In Western philosophy, man is the centre of the world whereas in the Eastern philosophy man is as at the periphery. The word *parivāra* literally means that what is seen from the *paridhi* (periphery). Thus self-importance which is very much a norm in the West, is the antithesis of Eastern philosophy of *parivāra* or family.

There may be naturally legitimate reasons for the selfish philosophy in the West, primarily due to the climatic extremities, limited availability of food, and need for protection against cold weather, especially during the Ice Age. Their approach to survival perhaps leads them to remain selfish. For example, most of North America and Europe still get only one crop in contrast to India where three crops are easily possible. Thus the behaviour of the Western world is understandable, but it cannot be condoned in today's world, and can certainly not be applicable to other cultures and geography (particularly in the southern hemisphere of the world) when understood correctly and applied properly.

Cautions are advised even for the use of Western science in other cultures for fear of misunderstanding and conflict for local cultures and traditions. Professor Northrop of Yale University pointed this out while writing the *Introduction to the Physics and Philosophy* (Prometheus Books, 1999) of Werner Heisenberg who had received Nobel Prize in 1932 for quantum mechanics. Professor Northrop wrote:

- The instruments of modern science derive from its theory and require a comprehension of that theory for their correct use.
- This theory rests on philosophical as well as physical assumptions.
- When comprehended, these philosophical assumptions generate a personal and social mentality and behaviour quite different from, at points incompatible with, the family, caste and tribally centred mentality of native Asian, Middle Eastern or African people.

Family and Culture

These observations suggest that if something as concrete as physics may be affected by the philosophy and culture, then more pliable topics like family relationship ought to be influenced by cultural experience and philosophy. Indian experience and philosophy must therefore be considered when examining families. And given the experience of the world in maintaining family structure, as shown in Table 1 below, it is more important that the philosophy underpinning the stable Indian marriages (India does not even appear on the list of countries with most divorce rates) be examined and perhaps highlighted.

Table 1: Divorce Rates of all Countries, Compared to US

Country	Divorce Rate (Per 1000 population per year)	Rate as per cent of US Rate
Sri Lanka	0.15	3.03
Brazil	0.26	5.25
Italy	0.27	5.45
Mexico	0.33	6.67
Turkey	0.37	7.47
Mongolia	0.37	7.47
Chile	0.38	7.68
Jamaica	0.38	7.68
Cyprus	0.39	7.88
El Salvador	0.41	8.28
Ecuador	0.42	8.48
Mauritius	0.47	9.49
Thailand	0.58	11.72
Syria	0.65	13.13
Panama	0.68	13.74
Brunei	0.72	14.55
Greece	0.76	15.35
China	0.79	15.96
Singapore	0.80	16.16

Tunisia	0.82	16.57
Albania	0.83	16.77
Portugal	0.88	17.78
Korea	0.88	17.78
Trinidad and Tobago	0.97	19.60
Qatar	0.97	19.60
Guadeloupe	1.18	23.84
Barbados	1.21	24.44
Finland	1.85	37.37
Canada	2.46	49.70
Australia	2.52	50.91
New Zealand	2.63	53.13
Denmark	2.81	56.77
United Kingdom	3.0	62.22
Russia	3.36	67.88
Puerto Rico	4.47	90.30
US	4.95	100.00

(http://www.divorcereform.org/nonus.html)

Source: Statistics provided by "Fathers' Manifesto" <fathers9@idt.liberty.com> in posting to familylaw-l@lawlib.wuacc.edu, I believe their source was a World Almanac or something similar from 1994 or thereabouts.

Indian philosophy in general has been multiculturalistic, which is the reflection of two golden goals of life for any living being. These are independence and freedom. Within India, there are differences in practices of marriage ceremonies irrespective of language, religion, and in many cases even region. However, ultimately the goal is for the stability of the family. Rituals and traditions vary with *jāti/kula/varṇa*, and also depend on the educational, financial, and social status of the families involved, and urban vs. rural location of the families.

Indian society is currently undergoing major transition due to economic progress and educational achievements. The traditional values are therefore under natural stress. While arranged marriage still makes over 99 per cent marriages in India, young people, particularly those living in cities and more exposed to Western values, tend to feel liberated and at times pursue what is called "love" marriage. Whether such marriages are "love" or "lust" based, there is a tendency to fall into catchy phrases like "falling in love", or "love is blind" which more often than not leads young and restless to a path sometimes at odds with the families.

In recent years, there have been dire consequences of young deciding to marry on their own, especially if the couples are from different *jāti*s or religions. There have been family tensions, at times leading to "honour killings". There are communities like *Khāp*s of Haryana state who have taken a political stand to force governments to ban same *gotra* marriages. Educated liberal class in India is aghast at such stands, but traditions are not easily done away with.

Family Traditions and Government

Traditions can also take ugly forms, such as dowry system, which can make family lives of the women anguished and intolerable. Despite the laws against dowry, the menace continues to grow in Indian society. Government response to enact further laws to protect women has also taken an ugly turn, and is being used to settle scores between families.

Clearly, enacting laws, particularly with selfish culture in mind, is not a very effective approach to solve social and family problems. However, Government of India has gone on with several intriguing laws to solve family problems. Interestingly, these laws are enacted only for Hindus, the majority community in India, leaving Muslims and Christians untouched presumably to exhibit the government's secular practice. In addition to giving an impression of Hindu practices in need of reforms (thereby wrong), the secular principles borrowed from West where culture and practices are very different are being applied to Indian culture, many times confusing the population, and also at times at the behest of international organizations and groups.

Some of the recent laws or government positions are listed below:

1. Government of India enacted a law that children are liable to take care of parents, and can be sued by parents if they default.
2. Parents cannot sell inherited properties without children's consent.
3. Live-in relationship is fine, citing Rādhā and Kṛṣṇa as example of live-in relationship.
4. Girls and boys of less than 16 years of age can have sexual relationship even though marriage age is 18 years for girls and 21 years for boys.

These laws and assertions are obviously anti-family and anti-Indian culture, and unfortunately applied selectively to Hindu population. Even Supreme Court judges took the government to task on the selective application of amendments to Hindus.

The Supreme Court of India said that government's attempts to reform personal laws don't go beyond Hindus who have been more tolerant of such initiatives (*The Times of India*, 11 February 2011; http://timesofindia.indiatimes. com/articleshow/7456761.cms?prtpage=1).

> The Hindu community has been tolerant to these statutory interventions. But there appears a lack of secular commitment as it has not happened for other religions.

Justices Dalveer Bhandari and A.K. Ganguly made the observation while hearing petitions filed by the National Commission for Women and its Delhi chapter. The petitioners had sought formulation of a uniform marriageable age and complained that different stipulations in as many statutes had created confusion.

In fact, the Hindu Marriage Act of 1955 itself is fairly arbitrarily done, and has almost nothing to do with Hindu philosophy or general practices. At least no references are made to any Hindu scriptures, consultation, or consensus. Government continues to make laws for Hindus without even a shred of consideration to either the community or its religious authorities. Many a time Hindu related laws are singled out to be enacted at the behest of a few elite class experiences, international pressure, domestic politics, or to create equivalence to other communities, viz. Christians and Muslims, both communities having extensive references to the social and legal aspects in their religious books, unlike Hindu texts.

It is certainly true that Hindu texts are more of guidance at spiritual, intellectual, and social levels, and allow flexibility for time and place. Nevertheless, a secular government, with a society less inclined to be intellectually engaged at mass level, and much less being sought to provide philosophical input to the provisions, is committing a grave long-term mistake in imposing Western practices on its people. This acquires more significance and importance when one considers the diversity that the Hindu community exhibits traditionally, which has continued with many of the practices of the only ancient living civilization.

Obviously, there is a major disconnect between the society and the rulers. India is a very large society with many of the cultural intermixes to be ruled by a single set of laws and provisions. India and Hindu represent a diversity of thoughts and practices that is integral to its existence. There is no reference in ancient India to have a constitution, judges, advocates, as wide ranging as it is currently enforced. It has been a self-policing society, governed by *kuladharma, jātidharma, varṇadharma, rāṣṭradharma,* and *paramadharma*. Currently, such things are not even seriously considered while making policies and laws for the society.

There are many ills that are creeping in the Indian society, as a result of not considering the traditions, practices, and ancient wisdom in making policies and laws by the politicians and bureaucrats, and in the enforcement by the police and judiciary. It is, therefore, essential to bring the issue of the Indian family system to at least a certain level of intellectual and scholarly debate. It is hoped that this exercise will spill over into the policy debates and eventually in the society for charting its course for future.

Scholarship of Family System

In this effort, a gathering of over a dozen scholars from India and United States in the summer 2006 took a comprehensive stock of the social and family conditions in the world, and developed a consensus that an all-encompassing development and peace in society is only possible with the time-tested value system of joint family.

While decrying the custom of paying dowry and the ever increasing greed of society, Divya Tripathi of DAV College of Girls, Haryana, India, speaking on the Vedic Philosophy of Marriage propounded that "the entire thrust of Vedic philosophy is to attain worldly happiness and spiritual upliftment as the goal of life."

Citing Vedas, Tripathi outlined that the way to achieve the goals of life is to scrupulously follow the four *āśrama*s or stages of life, of which *gṛhasthāśrama* (householder stage) is given the highest status. The backbone of the *gṛhasthāśrama* is marriage, which has attracted the most elaborate descriptions from Vedas to various Smṛtis (memoirs of great sages and rulers) and Purāṇas, the ancient historical accounts of Indian traditions.

"Any relationship must bring out growth and harmony at the individual, family, and society levels, otherwise it would not work," said Professor Madhu Jhaveri in his presentation on Integrating Principles of a Hindu Family System. And, the growth should involve physical or material, mental or intellectual, and spiritual. Jhaveri pointed out that marriage or husband-wife relationship should be looked at from this point of view.

Despite strong tradition of joint family system in India, major shifts in attitudes are taking place even in India, where at least in cities and towns nuclearization of families is taking place. According to Professor V.T. Patil, "the joint family system which has established its resilience over a long period in Indian history may undergo a major transformation in the light of momentous systemic developments like the impact of modernization, globalization, liberalization, and science and technology."

The fact that breaking of the joint family in India is afoot is obvious from the number of elderly people being placed in "pay and stay homes." According to Jyotsna Kalavar of Penn State University, there is a tremendous increase in the elderly population in such institutions in India. She attributed this change to "dual career families, changing values, and nuclear family dynamics."

An interesting observation made by Professor Kalavar with elderly people living in pay-and-stay homes in Chennai area was that they had more contacts with their daughters than sons, which "appears to be a departure from traditional expectations placed on the male child for provision of late life care." However, a question remains whether less contact with sons is due to a negative role played by the daughter-in-law.

Speaking in support of the joint family system, Mona Khaitan, a professor of business in MassBay Community College, presented data suggesting the joint family system fares better economically. According to the National Family Health Survey of 1998-99, while joint families form only 35 per cent of the low income households, they form 53 per cent of the high income households.

Professor Khaitan explained the better economic success of the joint family as it "enjoys the economies of scale; the costs are lower than if two or three households were to be maintained, making for increased income."

In addition to the economic advantage, Professor Khaitan advanced the idea of "relational wealth", originally proposed by late Professor Romesh Diwan of Rensselaer Polytechnic College in Troy, NY. This is intangible wealth amassed that promotes physical, emotional, intellectual, and psychic well-being of each individual.

Writing in an article entitled "Gandhian Economics: An Empirical Perspective" in 2001, Professor Diwan had written that "it (relational wealth) is a state where people live together in families of blood relations or of friends, where commitments are made and kept, where one's greatest pleasure is to see that the other person is satisfied and happy."

Rabi Mishra, an economist at Harvard University at that time, emphasized that many of the philosophical underpinnings of Indian society "are ingrained in various customs and rituals observed by a typical family across the twelve months of a year." He, however, warned that "human race is at a critical juncture now with material desires trying to reign over its mind. The march towards self-destruction is on. It is time one remembers and relearns the ethics of Indian family system to set the drowning ship in order."

That warning may turn out to be literally true, according to the article by Bal Ram Singh, included in these proceedings. He presented data from published journal articles which predicts that "There is sound scientific evidence to suggest that by living in a supportive family environment there is substantial personal growth, both physical and mental. Studies have shown that a joint family system is helpful to patients in health and health care of individuals' several diseases. Many of the practices at the societal level (such as marriage), although under substantial pressure in modern times, find scientific backing from neuroscience and genetics."

Sociologist V.D. Misra of Lucknow University presented the history, fundamentals, and objectives of Indian family system in the context of future as the global family system or *vasudhaivakuṭumbakam*.

Modernization and globalization while present a great challenge to maintain in the face of need and desire for mobility, separation, and individualism, there is also a greater understanding of global issues of environmental erosion and natural living. There are social challenges to maintain the essence of joint family system in modern world.

Honorable C.M. Bhandari, a former Indian ambassador to several countries, including United Arab Emirates, Cambodia, and Poland, used his personal example to suggest that the idea of joint family can be practised effectively in today's world.

A critical point made by several of the scholars was the leadership of women in family affairs. Divya Tripathi quoted *Mahābhārata* to say "the house is not the home, the mistress of the house is called the home."

According to Tripathi, the value of traditional value system and status of women got badly affected with the passage of time because of reasons like political and cultural invasions, urbanization, industrialization, changed socio-economic conditions, etc.

To complete the issues related to the Indian family system in its element of intellectual conditioning, a chapter on "Gārhasthya (household), The Supreme Moral Ideal: A Path to Śreyas (Ought)" was invited from D.R. Satapathy of Utkal University, India. This chapter provides philosophical rationale in practical terms how to approach *preyas* (likable or pleasurable) and *śreyas* (what ought to be). He, along with Gautama Satapathy, Lecturer in Zakir Hussein College of University of Delhi, weaves through concepts of Indian ethical nuances such as *śreyas, preyas, svadharma, tapaḥ, ācāra, śraddhā, puruṣārtha, lokasaṁgraha, sthitaprajña,* and their role and the position in the Indian *āśrama* of *gārhasthya* extending its domain by inevitability to civilization, culture, history, moral, social and spiritual life, including society and governance.

Future Prospects of Indian Family System

Problems such as dowry and female foeticide have made inroads in the Indian society. Politics and policies have made inroads in not only taking care of problems but also in perfectly private affairs of the families. A crack is becoming visible in the Indian family system. Fortunately, most of the Western world has had bad experience with their family life for a few decades, and there is slow but sure move towards more stable families.

A coincident has been the spread of Yoga and Āyurveda in the Western world, particularly in the United States. More and more Westerners are learning more about true traditions of India, something Indians themselves have forgotten or have little understanding of. There are cases of American couples getting married in Vedic traditions. In addition, Non-Resident Indians, who tend to follow their traditions a bit more seriously than Indians back in India, are also learning the meanings of their culture and traditions better. This development combined with the penchant of resident Indians for all that comes from the Western world may reinforce the fundamental values of Indian family system.

There is so much misunderstanding about India's traditions, especially their scholarly analysis, both in India and abroad. This book is intended to be a small step in the direction of clearing some of those misunderstandings.

1- Conference opening with *Śaṅkhanāda* (conch-blowing)

2 - Marcie Williams

2a - Marcie Williams, Senior Vice-President, University of Massachusetts, inaugurating the Conference

3 - Makaranad Paranjape of Jawaharlal Nehru University
raising a question at the Symposium

The Times of India. Yoga "couples" fly from US in India to get married, *Source*: Viju B, TNN 6 October 2009.

1

Vedic Philosophy of Marriage

Divya Tripathi

Human Race and its Goal of Life

HUMANS are considered the supreme creation in Indian philosophy[1] because they possess the highest intellect, faculties of making judgement and creative imagination. In fact, they are considered to be very much a part of the supreme divine. Scholars from all over the world have been striving hard to understand and visualize the goal of life since ages. This purpose is much beyond the epicurean theory of eat, drink and be merry. As against this, Vedic philosophy aims at attaining worldly happiness (*abhyudaya*) as also spiritual upliftment (*niḥśreyasa*). In other words, it is to achieve all the four, i.e. *dharma, artha, kāma, mokṣa,* popularly known as *puruṣārtha catuṣṭaya*.[2]

In order to realize this goal, the Vedic sages have taken great care in prescribing a course of conduct for day-to-day life. The *āśrama* system is one such course, which is unique in itself. Smr̥tis have mentioned that there are four *āśramas*: *brahmacarya, gr̥hastha, vānaprastha* and *saṁnyāsa*.[3] Dharmaśāstras

---

1. *na mānuṣāt śreṣṭhataram hi kiñcit* | — *Mahābhārata*, Śānti Parva, 299.20

2. *dharmārthakāmamokṣaśca puruṣārtha udāhr̥tāḥ* |
— *Viṣṇu Purāṇa*, 1.18.21

3. *brahmacārī gr̥hasthaśca vānaprastho yatistathā* |
ete gr̥hasthaprabhavāścatvāraḥ pr̥thagāśramāḥ | — *Manu-Smr̥ti*, 6.87

recommend that one should follow *āśrama*s in the order[4] in which they have been prescribed. Thus, taking the life expectancy as 100 years, it has been divided into four parts of 25 years each. In the first part, a man is to spend his life in the house of the *guru* (life of a student), i.e. *brahmacarya;* the second part is meant to live a householder's life with his wife (married life), *gṛhastha;* in the third part, he is to spend time in the forest (retired life), i.e. *vānaprastha* and in fourth part he is to live a life of a wanderer, fully detaching himself from the worldly tie (religious wanderer[5]), i.e. *saṁnyāsa.*

This distribution of the whole span of a person's life into four different stages is very important as it allows a person to pursue all the *puruṣārtha*s (life's objects) concerning this world and the world beyond.

Of all the *āśramas*, *gṛhasthāśrama* is given the highest significance. Manu says,

> As rivers, great and small, find a resting place in the ocean, even so men of all *āśrama*s gather their stability and support at the hands of the householder.[6]
>
> Since men in the three other *āśrama*s are daily supported by the householder with sacred knowledge and food, the householder's is the leading *āśrama.*[7]

---

4. *sarve 'pi kramaśastvete yathāśāstra niṣevitāḥ* | — *Manu-Smṛti*, 6.88
5. *caturthamāyuṣo bhāgamuṣitvādhyaṁ gurau dvijaḥ* |
dvitīyamāyuṣo bhāgaṁ kṛtadāro gṛhe vaset | |
vaneṣu ca vihṛtyaivaṁ tṛtīyaṁ bhāgarmāyuṣaḥ |
caturthamāyuṣo bhāgaṁ tyaktvā saṅgāt parivrajet | |
— *Manu-Smṛti*, 4.1, 6.33
6. *yathā nadīnadāḥ sarve sāgare yānti saṁsthitim* |
tathaivāśramiṇaḥ sarve gṛhasthe yānti saṁsthitim | |
— *Manu-Smṛti*, 6.90
7. *yasmātrayo 'pyāśramiṇo jñānenānnena cānvaham* |
gṛhasthenaiva dāryante tasmājjyeṣṭhāśramo gṛhī | |
— *Manu-Smṛti*, 3.78

In accordance with the precepts of the Veda and the Smṛti, the householder is declared to be superior to all of them.[8]

Gautama described it as "the source of other *āśrama*s because others do not produce offsprings".[9]

In general, since each *āśrama* is regarded as an essential stage for the development of individual, all are important. Yet, the *gṛhasthāśrama* has been glorified, not in terms of absolute superiority of the *āśrama* over all others, but from the point of view of the "social values" of this *āśrama*. It is exalted because firstly, it lends support to the other three *āśrama*s; secondly, it provides the ground for practising and cultivating all the three *puruṣārtha*s, that is, *dharma, artha* and *kāma*; thirdly, it provides the stage to discharge the three obligations (*ṛṇa*s) the debt to the gods (*deva-ṛṇa*), to the ancestors (*pitṝṇa*) and to the sages (*ṛṣi-ṛṇa*), and fourthly, it is the period when he fulfils all his social obligations.

Marriage in one form or the other is prevalent in all the societies of the world for social order. In the Indian culture too, the foundation of the *gṛhastha* (family) is "marriage" which has existed since ancient times. The Vedic philosophy dwells in detail in the physical, mental, social, religious and spiritual importance of marriage in the life of a man.

The world today faces many problems relating to marriage and family life. In the absence of social restrictions and self-control, young boys and girls, attracted by opposite sex, are indulging in pre-marital sex activities at the tender age, resulting in unwanted pregnancies and abortions. Even marital life is becoming unstable day by day as more and more marriages are solemnized out of infatuation and lust, devoid

8. *sarveṣāmapi caiteṣāṁ vedasmṛtividhānataḥ* |
gṛhastha ucyate śreṣṭhaḥ sa trīnetānbibharti hi | | — *Manu-Smṛti*, 6.89

9. *teṣam gṛhastho yoniraprajanatvaditaresam* |
— *Gautama-Dharma-Sūtra* (GDS), 1.3.3

of mutual love, emotional bonding, compassionate feelings and a sense of responsibility for each other. Religious and social restraints are lacking to check their irrational behaviour, with the result that there is an alarming increase in cases of divorce resulting in disturbed family life, separated families and increasing number of children with psychological problems. Apart from this, dowry deaths are still prevalent in India and even the wives are being killed in Western countries to claim huge insurances — a result of materialistic needs. There is no proper code of conduct to fix their dos and don'ts. In fact, rules are being framed to legalize their whimsical and unethical activities. For instance the gay marriages in UK, Canada, etc. have since been made legal, though such unions are only perversions and hence are going to be harmful at a later stage individually and socially. Thus, despite the materialistic progress, instead of contentment, peace and bliss there is distrust, unrest, frustration, selfishness, insecurity, tensions and stresses in the society.

The analytic study of Vedic philosophy of marriage and family holds a ray of hope in this grim situation. In Vedic tradition, marriage happens to be a sacramental rite. In it, two complementary halves are brought together to make a whole.[10] *Taittirīya Brāhmaṇa* says:

> He, indeed, is without sacrifice who has got no wife." It again adds "He is himself a half man, the second half is wife."[11]

It is a union of two bodies, minds and souls that lovingly resolve to live together. According to the Śāstric view, the spiritual aspect of marriage is so important that the husband

---

10. *tasmādardhaṁ vṛgalamiva sva iti smāha yājñavalkya* |
— *Śatapatha Brāhmaṇa*, 14.4.2.4-5

11. *ayajñiyo vā eṣa yo 'patnīkaḥ* | — *Taittirīya Brāhmaṇa*, 2.2.2.6
atho arddho vā eva ātmanaḥ yatpatnīḥ | — *Taittirīya Brāhmaṇa*, 2.9.4.7

is said to have received his life partner as chosen by/from God and not as per his own choice. The Vedas quoted:

> I take thy hand for good fortune, that thou mayest attain old age with me as thy husband, the gods have given thee to me that I may be the master of the household.[12]

The Aims of Marriage

Three major objectives of marriages have been highlighted in the Vedic text:

DHARMA

Vedic tradition regarded *dharma* (the performance of religious rites and righteous duties) as the first and the highest aim of marriage life. Vedas and Smṛtis declare that religious rites and *śrāddha* must be performed by the couple together[13] as such ceremonies are incomplete without the participation of wife[14] and, thus, are fruitless if done alone by a man.[15] Considering this, sage Kaśyapa has suggested marrying a suitable pure girl.[16] Pāṇini has emphasized a woman, who helps her husband in the performance of sacrificial acts, *yajña*, is called *patnī*[17] (wife).

PRAJĀ (PROGENY)

It is a Vedic belief that from his very birth a man owes three debts — *brahmacarya* (study of Vedas) to the sages (*ṛṣi-ṛṇa*),

---

12. *grabhaṇāmi te saubhāgyāya hastaṁ* |
mayā patyā jaradaṣṭiryathasaḥ | | — *ṚV*, X.85.36
13. *grabhaṇāmi te saubhāgyāya hastam* |
mayā patyā jaradaṣṭīryāsaḥ | | — *Manu-Smṛti*, 9.87, *ṚV*, X.85.36
14. *Śatapatha Brāhmaṇa*, 5.1.6.10.
15. *naikayāpi vinā kāryamādhānaṁ bhāryayā dvijaiḥ* |
akṛtaṁ tadvijānīyāt sarvānvācārabhavanti yat | | — *Kātyāyana*, 8.5
16. *dārādhīnāḥ kriyā śarvā brāhmaṇānāṁ viśeṣaṭaḥ* |
dārān sarvapratyanena viśuddhānudvahettataḥ |
— *Kṛtyakalpataru* (Vivāha Prakaraṇa)
17. *Pāṇini-Sūtra*, 4.1.33.

sacrifice to the gods (*deva-ṛṇa*) and progeny to ancestors (*pitṝṇa*).[18] Therefore, after the end of *brahmacarya āśrama*, the graduate is directed to enter into a marriage alliance with a suitable girl for procreation.[19] There are several *mantras* referring to prayers for progeny.[20] So much so that a man is said to become immortal by giving birth to children.[21]

RATI (CONJUGAL HAPPINESS)

In Indian tradition *kāma* is considered one among the four *puruṣārthas*. *Kāma* refers to all the innate desires and urges of man including sex and its understanding. This *kāma* legitimately is to be fulfilled through marriage.[22] Manu mentions that *kāma* is one of the goals of marriage. Vātsyāyana points out that in his young age, a man should seek to satisfy his natural craving for enjoyment and pleasure (*kāma*).[23] But, Kauṭilya has clearly cautioned that *kāma* should be governed by *dharma*.[24]

The ancient sages were aware of the biological needs of a man. Therefore, they wrote:

> Sex urge is common in man and animal but *dharma* distinguishes man's instinct from that of an animal by putting restraints on desires.[25]

---

18. *jāyamāno vai brāhmaṇastribhirṝṇavāṁ jāyate brahmacaryeṇa ṛṣibhyo yajñena devebhyoḥ prajñayā pitṛbhyaḥ* I — *Taittirīya Saṁhitā*, 6.3.10.5
19. *prajātantuṁ mā vyavacchetsīḥ* I — Ibid: 1.11.1, *Ap.DS*, 2.5.11.12
20. *ṚV*, I.91.13, 20; III.1.123, *Atharvaveda*, 11.1.21.
21. *udehi vediṁ prajayā vardhayaināṁ* I
prajāmanu prajāyase tadu te martyā 'mṛtamiti I I — *Ap.DS*, 2.9.24.1
22. *apatyaṁ dharmakāryāṇi śuśrūṣā ratiruttamā* I
dārādhīnastathā svargaḥ pitṝṇāmātmanaśca ha I I — *Manu-Smṛti*, 9.28
23. *Kāmasūtra*, 1.2.14.
24. *Arthaśāstra*, 1.7.3.
25. *āhāra-nidrā-bhaya maithunaśca sāmānyametatpaśubhirnarāṇām* I
dharmo hi teṣāmdhiko viśeṣo dharmeṇa hīnāḥ paśubhiḥ samānāḥ I I
— *Mahābhārata*, Śānti Parva, 294.29

4 - Divya Tripathi, DAV College of Girls, Haryana, India

4a - Divya Tripathi, presenting her paper

There is nothing unwholesome or guilty about the sex life. Lord Kṛṣṇa described himself as *kāma*, which is not against the tenets of *dharma*.[26] Sensual love is thus sublimated when in tune with *dharma*.

As against this concept of *dharma* in marriage, the modern concept of marriage lays more stress on conjugal happiness. The famous sociologist Mendoek, who after making comparative studies of marriage system of 250 groups, has concluded that objectives of marriage are primarily conjugal happiness, socio-economic co-operation and rearing of children.

A comparison of these two ways of looking at marriage and the resultant social set-up makes it amply clear as to how they immensely affected the social life and are responsible for the contemporary social behaviour. The Vedic times had a peaceful social life because of stable and satisfied married life. As against this, the modern society is facing great problems relating to sex abuse, dissatisfied married life and increasing number of divorces, etc. In Vedic marriage tradition, conjugal happiness was given the last place and that too governed by *dharma* and juxtaposed with control. But, in present-day society, *kāma* is given top priority in married life. This has resulted in bringing out an undisciplined progeny having crude values, defective virtues and inhuman behaviour. It has been proved that the thoughts and actions of a pregnant woman affect the body, mind and emotions of the unborn child. That is why, in India, today also, pregnant women are advised to lead a pure life by reading good and religious books and to avoid situations that upset their minds. For this very reason, even in the Western countries, scientists have warned pregnant women against smoking and drinking to avoid deformities in foetus.

---

26. *dharmāviruddho bhūteṣu kāmo 'smi bharatarṣabha* | — *Gītā*, 7.11

Eugenics

For continuation of qualitative human race, Smṛtis have exhorted people to judge the lineage, conduct, and characteristics of a man and a woman before they get married for having noble and worthy progeny, being one of the primary objectives of marriage.

ENDOGAMY

For this, Manu advises endogamy, i.e. marriage in one's own group (*varṇa*).[27] Such marriage will attract souls of similar nature. Vedic culture propounds many natural laws. First, it holds that a soul takes birth in a family that provides it the conducive environment for its evolution. A soul with *sattvika* element, for instance, is born in a family of brāhmaṇas and so on. Secondly, it considers that a child born to parents of same group (*varṇa*) inherits their biological, intellectual and moral traits. But, when there is a difference between the temperaments or the groups of the parents, the child tends to be like one parent or the other.[28]

HYPERGAMY

Hypergamy was recognized in ancient times, but not encouraged.

Anuloma

Dharmaśāstras allow *anuloma* marriage, i.e. to marry a girl from the lower caste, though such cases were not many and generally they were not held in high esteem. Manu has clearly declared:

> Among the twice-born, a girl of the same caste is commendable for wifehood, but for those who are given to

---

27. *udvahetadvijo bhāryāṁ savarṇāṁ lakṣaṇānvitām* I — *Manu-Smṛti*, 3.4

28. *sarvavarṇeṣu tulyāsu patnīṣvakṣatyoniṣu* I
ānulomyena saṁbhūtājātyā jñeyāsta eva te I I
— *MS*, 10.5

lust, girls from other castes can also be had in order.[29] But children born out of such marriages (*varṇasaṅkara*) were given low social status.[30] However, marriage with a śūdra girl was forbidden.[31]

Pratiloma

All the scriptures are against *pratiloma* marriage — marriage of a low caste man with a girl of higher class. But śūdra's marriage with a brāhmaṇa girl was considered scandalous.

EXOGAMY (MARRIAGE IN A DIFFERENT FAMILY AND LINEAGE)

In Vedic traditions, it is a firm belief that marriage partners should not be from the same family. To ensure that the man and the woman are not from the same *gotra* (lineage), it is customary even today to check the *gotra* before marriage. Smṛtis uphold that marriage within the family is irreligious, condemnable and sinful as it leads to the degeneration of the race.

It is suggested in *Manu-Smṛti* that five generations from the maternal side and seven from the paternal side must be avoided in marriages.[32] Marriages beyond these only are considered proper.

Willard C. Olson[33] had given the following scientific explanation that a child inherits 24 chromosomes from each parent or inherit 12 chromosomes from each grandparent, or

29. *savarṇāgre dvijātīno praśastā dārakarmaṇi |*
kāmatastu pravṛttānāmimāḥ syuḥ kramaśo 'varāḥ | | — *MS*, 3.12

30. *śūdrādāyogavaḥ kṣattā cāṇḍālaścādhamonṛṇām |*
vaiśyarājanyaviprāsu jāyante varṇasaṅkarāḥ | | — *MS*, 10.12

31. *MS*, 3.15-17.

32. *ūrdhvaṁ saptamātpitṛbandhubhyo bījinaśca mātṛbandhubhyaḥ pañcamāt |* — *MS*, 3.5; *G.DS*, 1.4.2-3

33. *Child Development*, p. 16, Boston: D.C., Health and Company, 1949.

an average of 6 from each great-grandparent or 3 from each great-great grandparent or an average of 1 or 2 from each great, great, great grandparent. We go back as far as great-great-great-great-grandparents. Thereafter, there are not enough chromosomes involved for us to have even one from each of these more remote ancestors.

Genetics confirm this belief. When parents are closely related, recessive genes, that control undesirable characteristics, dominate in the children, causing improper and defective development. On the contrary, when the couple hail from different families and lineage, the children are strong, healthy and normal.

Willard C. Olson had remarked that cousins are more likely than unrelated persons to be carrying similar genes. If any undesirable genes are present, then inter-marriages are likely to cause undesirable characteristics to appear in the offspring. Probably, few of us are so sure of the excellence of our heredity that marrying a cousin is to be recommended.[34]

Da win says:

> The consequence of close inter-breeding carried on for too long a time are, as is generally believed, loss of size, constitutional vigour and fertility, sometimes accompanied by a tendency of malformation.[35]

The latest research has proved that when the partners are closely related, children born thereof do not develop normally. Incidence of abortions, pregnancy related problems, still born children, heart problem and emotional problems are higher in such couples than in those who hail from different ancestors. Children of such couples have been routinely found to be

---

34. *Child Development*, p. 18.

35. *Variation of Animals and Plants under Domestication*, London, 1868.

suffering from mutation. The clinical features consist of progressive intellectual deterioration with varying degree of cerebral dysfunction, and seizures in some cases. Enlargement of the head is also a feature.[36]

Examination of the Family

In addition to the consideration of the caste and *gotra*, the particular families of the would-be couple were also thoroughly examined. *Āśvalāyana Gṛhya-Sūtra* clearly lays down that first of all, the family should be examined, both from the father's and mother's side.[37] Manu enjoins that "a man of a noble family, in order to increase the excellence of his own, should always make relations with members of noble families and should shun the ignoble."[38] He further explained that the most esteemed families were those who were noted for their good deeds, learning and morality. Those should always be made relatives, who are pure from their deeds; who are born in the good families and observe unbroken *brahmacarya*; who are related to noble families and have risen to eminence; who are contented, gentlemen, agreeable, saintly and equitable; who are devoid of greed, attachment, envy, pride and infatuations and those who are not given to anger and are always tranquil in their minds.[39]

Vigyaneshwar is of the opinion that the families of those are to be taken as good, who are famous from five generations,

---

36. Vidya Krishnan Quoting, I.C. Verma, *The Hindustan Times*, 26 January 2006.
37. *Āśvalāyana Gṛhyasūtra*,1.5, *kulamagre parīkṣeta mātṛta pitṛtaśceti* |
38. *uttamairuttamonityaṁ sambandhānācaretsadā* |
ninīṣuḥ kulamutkarṣamadhamānadhamāṁstyajet | |
39. *MS*, 3.6, 17.

both from mother's and father's sides, and are reputed for their *learning* and *character*.[40]

On moral and physical grounds, many families were prohibited. Manu says, these ten families, however rich they might be, should be avoided. They are: one without good deeds; without great men; without Vedas; hairy and suffering from piles; consumption; dysentery; epilepsy; white leprosy and leprosy proper. Families suffering from contagious disease should also be shunned.[41]

The moral objections were the following:

> Those families should be avoided with care, the members of which are thieves, cheats, impotent, atheists, living on objectionable means, deformed, always bringing enmity with brave persons, enemies of the state, cowards and ill-reputed.[42]

The reason for the utmost care taken for the examination of the family was primarily eugenic. The best possible progeny was desired and for it, physically, mentally and morally fit matches were necessary, as children inherit good or bad qualities of their parents. Emphasizing the point, Hārīta says that offsprings are born according to the families.[43] *Manu-Smṛti* mentions that:

> The good families fall to ill fame, etc. from bad marriages, disappearances of the religious duties and the non-study of the Vedas.[44]

---

40. *puruṣā ev ca pūruṣāḥ daśabhiḥ puruṣai mātṛtaḥ* |
pañcabhiḥ pitṛtaḥ pañcabhirvikhyātaṁ yatkulaṁ tasmāt | |
— *Vijñāneśvara* in *Yājñavalkya Smṛti*, 1.54

41. *MS*, 3.6-7.

42. *MS*.

43. *kulānurūpāḥ prajā sambhavanti* |
piturvā bhajate śīlaṁ maturvobhayameva vā | | — *VMS*, vol. II, p. 58

44. *MS*.

Thus, in order to save the families from degeneration, it has been repeatedly stressed that one has to be very cautious in selecting the match.

Qualifications of a Bride

Apart from family, Vedic text gives detailed instructions with regard to the selection of wife wherein personal qualifications were taken into account. Manu says, "let him wed a woman, who is free from bodily defects; who has an agreeable name, the graceful gait of a swan or an elephant, a moderate quantity of hair in the body and on the head, small teeth and soft limbs."[45] Yājñavalkya speaks in a general way that the bride should be *kāntā* or lovely.[46] *Śatapatha* explains further,

> Having married a girl whose voice is like that of a swan, whose colour is like that of a cloud, and whose eyes are sweet and reddish, a householder finds happiness.[47]

Vedic text also gives detailed instructions that one should not marry a woman who has beard or moustache on her face, nor one whose appearance is like that of a man and voice is hoarse, who always speaks satirically. Further it is exhorted that a wise man should not wed a girl whose eyelids do not fall, whose eyesight is lost, whose ankles are projected or prominent, whose cheeks are sunken, who has lost her lusture, whose hands and feet are very thin, whose teeth are widely spaced and whose mouth is horrible.[48] Apart from external qualifications, intellect has also been taken into consideration when it is written that "how could one put up with a woman without intellect?"[49]

45. *avyaṁgāṅgī saumyanāmnīṁ haṁsavāraṇagāminīm* |
tanulomakeśadaśanāṁ mṛdvaṅgīmudvahetstriyam | | — *MS*, 3.10

46. *Yājñavalkya-Smṛti*, 1.75.

47. Quoted in *Vīramitrodaya* (*VMS*), vol. II, p. 731.

48. *VMS*, vol.II, p. 731.

49. *aprajñeyayā hi kathaṁ saṁvāsaḥ* | — *Śatapatha Brāhmaṇa*, 1.2.5.16

The bride should be younger than the bridegroom. She should be a potential mother as the main purpose of marriage is procreation.

Qualifications of a Bridegroom

The qualifications of a bridegroom were equally high. Yājñavalkya says that a bridegroom should possess all the good qualities of a bride.[50] The first requirement of a bridegroom was the completion of his *brahmacarya*.[51] In the opinion of the *Varāha Gṛhya-Sūtra,* a bridegroom should have subdued his anger and be cheerful in his spirits.[52] Other considerations were *wealth, looks, learning, intellect* and *family status*. Gautama says that the bride should be given to "a man who possesses learning, character, friends and modesty."[53] Yama lays down the most comprehensive qualifications of a bridegroom. "Having considered the family, character, physique, age, learning, wealth and resourcefulness, a wise man should give his daughter to him, there is nothing else to be considered."[54]

As against this, today, the vital determining factors of marriage are wealth and social status of the bridegroom, the other factors, which were important in Vedic way of life, being redundant.

Forms of Marriage

In Vedic tradition usually there have been eight types of marriage:

---

50. *etaireva guṇairyuktaḥ* | — *Yaj.S.*, 1.55

51. *vedanadhītya veduva vedam vāpi yathākramam* |
aviluptabrahmacaryo gṛhasthāśramamavaset | | — *MS*, 3.2

52. *vinītakrodhaḥ saharṣaḥ saharṣāṁ bhāryāṁ vindeta* |
— *Vārāha-Gṛhya Sūtra*, 10.1, 10.6

53. *vidyācāritryabandhuśīlasampannāya kanyāṁ dadyāt* | — *GauDS*, 1.4.4

54. *kulaṁ ca śīlaṁ ca vapurvayaśca vidyāṁ ca vittaṁ ca sanāthatāñca* |
etānguṇānsapta parīkṣya deyā kanyā budhaiḥ śeṣamacintanīyam | |
— *VMS*, vol. II, p. 754

BRĀHMA MARRIAGE

In *brāhma* marriage the father used to give away his daughter, specially dressed and adorned, to a man learned and good conduct, whom he himself invited.[55] This was supposed to be the purest form of marriage and might have been widely prevalent, as is exemplified by the marriage of Sūrya.

DAIVA MARRIAGE

In *daiva* marriage, the bride, beautifully adorned was offered by the parents to the priest and the marriage was solemnized during the course of sacrament.[56]

ĀRṢA MARRIAGE

The father gave away his daughter, and in return, according to the rule, he received from the bridegroom a cow and a bull as a promise that he would abide by the sacred laws of the Śāstras for keeping the marriage. Manu[57] and Vīramitrodaya[58] comment that such exchange was done in obedience to Vedic marriage laws and not with the idea of getting it as a price of the girl, out of greed.

PRĀJĀPATYA

This marriage is celebrated by the bride's father on receiving an assurance from the bridegroom that he and his bride will live together in conformity with *dharma*.[59]

---

55. *ācchādya cārcayitvā ca śrutiśīlavate svayaṁ* |
āhūya dānaṁ kanyāyā brāhmo dharmaḥ prakīrtitaḥ | |
— *GauDS*, 1.4.4; MS 3.27

56. *yajñe tu vivate samyagṛtvije karma kurvate* |
alaṅkṛtya sutādānaṁ daivaṁ dharmaṁ pracakṣate | | — *MS*, 3.28, *GDS*, 1.4.7

57. *MS*, 3.54.

58. *dharmanimitto hyasau sambandho na lobhanimittakaḥ* | — *VMS*, I, p. 822

59. *saha dharmaṁ carata iti prājāpatyaḥ* | — *Ash.GrS*, 1.6

This form required a free society where there was no seclusion of womenfolk and the bridegroom came forward to ask for the hand of the bride. This envisaged marriages among grown-ups who could understand the implications of the bond they were going to enter. This form of marriage fell into disuse when child marriages became in vogue.

ASURA MARRIAGE

In this marriage, the bridegroom gave as much wealth as he could afford to the girl as also to her father before he took her as his bride.[60] This type of marriage was condemned as it was construed to be the sale of the bride. It was considered that the lady so purchased could not attain the status of a wife and hence, not entitled to share the worship of gods and ancestors. She could only be a maidservant.[61] Moreover, such persons who give their daughters out of greed were taken to be sellers of their own selves and hence considered sinners. It was believed that they were doomed to hell and were destined to lose the pious deeds (*puṇya*) of their seven preceding generations.[62]

There are some references where the guardian of the girl had to offer dowry to the bridegroom. A girl who had some physical defects, was to be given in marriage with money.[63] In the *Aitareya Brāhmaṇa* a bargain marriage is called *paśuvivāha*[64] (animal marriage). But it is not clear as to which party extracted money.

---

60. *vittenā 'natiḥ strīmatāmasuraḥ* | — *GDS*, 1.4.9
61. *krītā dravyeṇa yā nārī na sā patnī vidhīyate* |
na sā daive na sā pitṛye dāsīṁ tāṁ kavayo viduḥ | | — *Bau.D.S.*, 1.11.21.4
62. Ibid., 1.11.21.5.
63. *ṚV*, X.23.11.
64. *Aitareya Brāhmaṇa*, 1.16.

GANDHARVA MARRIAGE

The *gandharva* marriage is based on mutual consent[65] and can be compared with the modern love marriage. Romance and absence of ceremonial solemnization characterize this type. According to some authorities, this method was praiseworthy, as it proceeded from mutual attraction and love.[66] Kaṇva, the foster father of Śakuntalā says in the *Mahābhārata*, "the marriage of a desiring woman with a desiring man, though without religious ceremonies, is the best marriage."[67] But majority of Smṛtis discouraged it on religious and moral grounds. It was inferior to the first five forms of marriage, because it was performed without sacred rituals and originated from lust. There were also apprehensions as regards the stability of such marriage ties, because love being the determining factor in such marriages, the relation might or might not be lasting.

RĀKṢASA MARRIAGE

This was a marriage by seizure of a girl by force from her house while she wept and called for assistance, after her kinsmen and friends had been slain in battle or wounded and their houses broken.[68]

PIŚĀCA MARRIAGE

This was the lowest type.[69] The bride was overpowered, made helpless through drugs or drinks, and her mental faculties paralyzed.[70]

---

65. *icchantyāḥ svayaṁ saṁyogo gandharvaḥ* | — *GauDS*, 1.4.8
66. *gandharvanapyeke praśaṁsanti sarveṣām snehānugatatvāt* |
— *Bau.D.S.*, 1.11.20.16
67. *sakāmāyāḥ sakāmena nirmantraḥ śreṣṭha ucyate* |
— *Mahābhārata*, 4.94.60
68. *MS*, 3.33; *GauD*, 1.4.11.
69. *paiśācaścāṣṭamo 'dhamaḥ* | — *MS*, 3.34
70. *GDS*, 1.4.11; *MS*, 3.34.

Of these eight types of marriage, Gautama,[71] Manu, etc. approved the first four types and considered others inferior and blasphemous. It is believed that the sons born from first four types of marriages tend to be bright, radiant with knowledge of Vedas and respected by good men. Possessing good looks and qualities of head and heart and righteousness, they have pelf, fame and full enjoyment of life and they would live hundred years.[72] The sons born from first four types of marriages — *brāhma, daiva, prājāpatya* and *ārṣa* absolve the sins of 21 (10 generations of ancestors plus himself plus 10 generations of progeny), 15 (7 ancestors plus self plus seven descendants), 13 (6 ancestors plus self plus six descendants), 7 generations (3 ancestors plus self plus 3 descendants), respectively.[73] On the contrary, the children born from the type of other than these four marriages would be cruel, liars and disrespectful to Vedas and sacred law[74] (*Manu* 3.37-41).

In the first four types of marriages, the element of *kāma* is controlled by *dharma*; the intellectual and moral upliftment of the bridegroom is given importance, and the experience of the parents plays an important role in the selection of the suitable match for their daughter. Therefore, such marriages help in the growth of the couple.

Of all these types, none exists in its original form as of today. The passage of time has slowly brought transformations in all these types of marriages. While some have altogether disappeared, others have undergone radical changes. The *piśāca* marriage was rarely practised even in ancient times. The *rākṣasa* marriage, though infrequently practised, was

71. *catvāro dharmyāḥ prathamāḥ* | — *GauDS*, 1.4.12-13

72. *MS*, 3.39-40.

73. *MS*, 3.38; 1.4, 26-27, *Yāj.S.* 1.58-60.

74. *GauDS*, 1.4.24.

prevalent among warrior class. The *asura* marriage is prevalent even today but largely among the people who stand very low on social hierarchy. *Ārṣa* and *daiva* forms of marriages have totally disappeared.

The prevalent form of marriage today is a modified form of *brāhma* marriage, in the sense that the father of the girl finds a suitable life partner for her and gives her as *dāna* (gift in the religious sense of the term) to the bridegroom. Of course, the custom of paying dowry, sometimes, a huge one, has extremely corrupted this type of marriage and has become a social bane.

Thus, earlier marriages were contracted not on the basis of individual choice, but according to the tenets of *kulācāra*, i.e. within permissible groups after fulfilling laid-down conditions.

The influence of the long foreign rule in India; the materialistic pursuits and successively increasing demand of dowry; the preference for highly paid bridegroom and the latest trend of globalization has slackened the hold of the Śāstric customs. However, restraint of *sagotra* (same lineage) marriages still applies. It is interesting to observe that whether it is an arranged or a love marriage, marriages among Hindu caste groups are being sanctified by performing marriage *saṁskāra* even today.

Dissolution of Vedic Marriage

In Indian culture, the marriage is a sacramental rite. The spiritual aspect of marriage was viewed so important that the husband was said to have received his wife from God and consequently, man and woman became integral part of each other making a whole. The Vedas say:

> Her bones become identified with his bones, flesh with flesh, skin with skin.

It is a holy union of mind, body and soul of the spouse and it is believed that even death does not put an end to it. It is considered to be the highest duty of husband and wife to remain united in marriage and be utterly faithful to each other.[75] Man must honour and protect his wife.

Since marriage is regarded as an eternal and sacred bond, which unites the husband and wife for the performance of their religious sacrifices, dissolution of marriage is, thus, not contemplated in Śāstras, for it is *adhārmika* (unreligious), unrighteous and sinful.

But later on, legal dissolution was allowed on any of the following grounds when a wife:

(a) Disrespects her husband, or
(b) Is passionate about someone else, or
(c) Drinks *madīrā* (liquor), or
(d) Is of bad conduct, or
(e) Is rebellious, or
(f) Is mischievous.

On the other hand, it was also held that woman should not be compelled to live with a mad husband, mentally defective man and eunuch or one afflicted with serious disease.

Conclusion

In all civilized societies amongst different social groups, a marriage in a family is recognized as the most significant aspect for the social well-being with child being the central figure. Due to rapid erosion and degradation of the norms and the tenets of the marriage institution, the society is heading towards total disintegration. To a great extent modern

75. *tathā nityaṁ yateyātāṁ strīpuṁsau tu kṛtakriyau |*
yathā nābhicaretāṁ tau viyuktāvitaretaram |
— *MS*, 9.101-102

conditions and lifestyle are responsible for dilution and erosion of the values. Life has become too hurried and materialistic. What needs to be done at this juncture to establish a healthy social order and promote peace and harmony in the society is to religiously practise Vedic values in the marriage institution with minor changes to make it amenable to the modern living conditions.

5 - Madhusudan Jhaveri of University of
Massachusetts Dartmouth, presenting his paper

2

Universal Values to Guide a Family

Madhusudan Jhaveri

This article is an attempt to discern the universal principles of harmonious and sustained family by going to the source and identifying common threads. It develops this by the use of history of nature and evolution. There are papers and essays written by others enumerating and describing the do's and dont's. There are also codes of Manu and others, and even the celebrated *Thirukkuraḷ* of Thiruvalluvar enumerating the aphorisms for a healthy and harmoniously functioning family. The requirements, which no one may disagree are (1) The family should be sustained, and held together, and (2) The members of the family must grow and develop to their full potential. The values discussed are universal, although their application to a family will be discussed. Some Sanskrit terms are used in describing these values for the benefit of those familiar with those. One may read the whole article neglecting the portions containing Sanskrit terms, without much loss. Otherwise, the essay would have been excessively long. This essay uses holistic, analytical and integral approach to discuss the subject.

Essential Cardinal Values of Growth and Harmony

A GREAT number of articles and papers are written to enumerate the values by which one can live. They are mostly written for a particular ethnic group or a particular religion, or even a particular culture. This essay is an attempt to unify those values transcending those religious, ethnic, and cultural boundaries. The contribution of this article is in making this subject of values to live by a universal one. And, whatever claims to be universal, must be of necessity, natural, i.e. evolved out of nature. Besides, it must be acceptable to the scientific community, and must also be universally true.

Therefore, this article attempts to unify the essential values of human life by relating them to common threads. It is presented before the intellectuals with all the modesty and humility. This writer is not aware of any other attempt by anyone made in this direction. The author would be obliged if it is brought to his attention.

The two most important, essential, and cardinal values this writer feels are (a) growth and (b) harmony. These two ultimate goals of life should not be controversial to any group. Growth is a natural process, but it should not be at the cost of others, a requirement for a peaceful coexistence. This requires harmonious functioning of the individuals without conflict as the goal.

Then to fulfil and adjust with respect to these two cardinal values, all other subordinate values can be derived, each and everyone satisfying the cardinal requirement of growth and harmony. Whichever value satisfies both the growth and harmony should be accepted as the universal value.

The next question to be answered is, how to recognize this growth? In order to gain some insight one has to refer to the science of natural evolution.

Growth: Science of Natural Evolution

THREE PHASES OF DEVELOPMENT

The life on this earth started with the unicellular organism, in the Proterozoic Era. A single cell developed in water and through a process documented and explained in the texts of natural history, through a phase which can be titled as "phase of physical development." This physical growth phase resulted into big animals like dinosaurs in Mesozoic Era.

The fossil bird also appeared towards the close of this era. Birds evolved further and it is believed that the "phase of mental development" came into being, with this evolution of birds. The expression of love by the birds towards their offspring was exhibited when the mother bird fed seeds to her babies. This phase was emotion-or mind-centred.

Then came the Cenozoic Era, the present "Age of Mammals." Latest arrival on the scene in Cenozoic Era is man. Man is characterized by his thinking or reasoning power as it has been also called "the age of reason" by others. Man is equipped with reasoning ability. So this phase has been called "Age of Reason," or "phase of intellect."

One feature one may note throughout this evolution, perhaps, is the first phase seems to be centred around "physical." The second phase which may be termed as emotion-centred, appeared when the birds evolved and their emotional attachment was exhibited in feeding the baby birds. This expression of love, which is an emotion, is also one characteristic of human beings in common with the birds. In addition to this emotion, human beings were also reasoning mammals as noted before. This "Phase of Reason or Phase of Intellect" happens to be the last phase, as variously documented and universally acknowledged by science.

PSYCHOSOMATIC PHASE

The phase after this is a specific psychosomatic centred phase in man. This centre, or action of this centre, is propelling human evolution beyond "the intellectual phase." This divine organ is naturally active in born sages, mystics, prophets and all men of genius and can be roused to activity with appropriate methods (*dhyāna-yoga*) in those already advanced on the path of evolution. It is worth noting at this point though, that the first three phases, namely physical, emotional, and intellectual were observed in history of nature in some measure. The last phase which was not named could be named as the "soul phase or spiritual phase." This phase even though is experienced by the sages, mystics or prophets is not commonly experienced by an ordinary man, though potentially all humans are capable of experiencing it, making it a universal. This universality should be called experiential rather than experimental to distinguish it from the initial three phases. Sometime in the not too distant future, it will be accepted by all, as the signs of such are already apparent on the world scene.

All this discussion is essential to delineate the growth indices. And one may come to conclusion that growth is from Physical → Mental → Intellectual → Spiritual.

The terms used in this paragraph may make sense only to readers of Indian origin. They are Sanskrit terms and can definitely be explained in English but would take lots of words and space. So only the terms are stated for the benefit of Indian readers who do not need the explanations.

Indian Terminology for Growth

Growth can also result by pursuing four *puruṣārtha*s (pursuits) discussed in the Indian ethics. They are called *dharma*, *artha*, *kāma*, and *mokṣa*. Growth automatically results by pursuing four *puruṣārtha*s.

Similarly Upaniṣads and *Gītā* describe *tamas* → *rajas* → *sattva*. (These three indices from lower (*tamas* to highest *sattva*) will result in growth.)

In Sanskrit terminology *vikṛti* → *prakṛti* → *saṁskṛti* will also result in growth.

Universal Innate Urges of Human Beings

There is yet another way of looking at man which can be universally acceptable, and that is looking at the innate urges present in humans. These common urges are rooted in the four faculties present in all human beings to a greater or smaller degree. All men possess a physical body. They all possess mind. They also have an intellect.

Besides these three faculties potentially all possess a soul or spirit. These four faculties have their own needs — physical needs, mental needs, intellectual needs and spiritual needs. By fulfilling the needs of all the four faculties the human being achieves total fulfilment. This could be termed as multi-centred growth (*sarvāṅgīṇa unnati* in Sanskrit).

Physically, body needs good nourishment, exercise, etc. Mentally or emotionally everyone needs respect, love or affection, etc. Intellect needs independent thinking, satisfaction of all curiosities, etc.

And spirit or soul of human beings needs peace. More developed a human being is more pronounced are the needs of the soul. A saint feels sympathy for the sufferings of others irrespective of his relation to them. Some are physical satisfaction-oriented, some are mental satisfaction-oriented, some are intellect-oriented and some spiritual orientation. Really speaking human beings pursue all or some of the four pursuits, partially.

First three types are not difficult to understand and accept for most of the thinking people but the fourth one, the spirit orientation or soul orientation is difficult for them to accept. To those, I ask a question: Why do you feel sorry for the people in suffering due to famine in a remote country? What connection do you have with those people? They are not your relatives, friends, or countrymen. The only explanation which comes to the mind is that your soul in some mysterious way is connected to them. There is also telepathic ability present in some which explains that somehow we may all be connected in some mysterious way.

Growth as Fulfilment of Innate Urges

Therefore in fulfilling the needs of these four innate urges human beings achieve growth. Fulfilling the needs of all the urges in a balanced way results in growth. Hindu thinkers have given four pursuits of human life for guiding this growth. They are not based on any narrow, irrational, reasoning; but on fully rational and logical analysis of human nature and universal principles of psychology.

These four pursuits are named in Sanskrit as (1) *dharma,* (2) *artha,* (3) *kāma,* (4) *mokṣa.* They contain all the four pursuits for fulfilment of innate urges of human beings. These are Sanskrit terms, and have nothing to do with any particular religion, as their basis is universal.

So far we have discussed growth aspect only, next let us look at the harmony aspect so essential for the topic of this essay.

Harmony

Harmony is essential for peaceful coexistence. Peaceful coexistence is also needed for growth of an individual in a catalytic sense, e.g. if there is no peace in the family, the growth of individuals, specially children in the family would be skewed.

Peace is really a by-product of harmony. If there is harmony in the family, there will be peace in the family, as its by-product. Peace is not an object itself. Therefore, all attempts of achieving peace, without worrying about harmony are fruitless. There has to be harmony between an individual and family, between family and community, between a community and greater society, between a society and a nation, between a nation and the world, between the world and nature, and finally between the nature and Almighty. Starting from an individual → to family → to community → to society → to nation → to world → to nature → to Almighty.

In Sanskrit there are four terms *vyaṣṭi* → *samaṣṭi* → *sṛṣṭi* → *parameṣṭhi* (for benefit of Indian readers).

Using these two cardinal values of growth and harmony all the secondary values can be derived or constructed. Harmony aspect can also be discussed from other points of view, but that could be left for a later date.

Thus far this article has discussed the two essential, cardinal values of growth and harmony, the remaining portion will be used to derive only some secondary values. These secondary values can be easily derived, keeping in mind the two cardinal requirements of growth and harmony. This endeavour can also be undertaken if scholars so desire. The following paragraphs are employed to the discussion of a few secondary values.

Some Secondary Values : Duty vs. Rights

Stress on duty rather than on rights results in harmony. Many theories stress rights as more important than duties, forgetting that duty is more fundamental than rights. Anyone can perform duty without depending on others. If there is no one to perform the duty, where would the rights be fulfilled from? You may go to a jungle, and still you can perform your duty. But who will supply your rights in a jungle? In fact, rights cannot exist without somebody doing his/her duty. In a family setting the duties of a man should include the rights of woman, children, and grandparents. Vice versa, the duties of a woman in the family should include the rights of in-laws, children, and husband. Family also has obligations towards society and even nature and animals. Kindness to animals and even trees and plants should be part of this duty. Duty orientation does not create conflict and results in harmony. We usually hear "fight for your rights," but we never even hear "fight for your duty." As you drive on left-hand side to minimize the accidents, especially front end collisions, this duty orientation in a family setting is conducive to harmony. Each one husband, wife everyone without exception must perform their duties to the best of their ability.

Sacrifice (Tyāga) vs. Selfish Orientation

Putting others first results in warmth in the family. You snatch something from others for yourself, that may give you material benefit, but does not give you warmth of affection. *Tyāga* is more conducive to harmony than selfishness.

DONATIONS TO A CHARITY OR A CAUSE

Usually what you give is surplus for you (there are exceptions though), that means it had diminished value for you (as per law of diminishing marginal returns), but for the receiver it had lot of value. By conventional economics this results in a greater benefit/cost ratio — of course, cost to you and benefit to someone other than you.

Selfish and individuality orientation isolates an individual and makes him more miserable but perhaps richer. Apparently what seems beneficial turns out to be a loss.

EXCELLENCE vs. COMPETITION

Stress on excellence rather than on competition. Excellence centred in you is self-motivated. So you are transformed into a spiritual and an exalted individual without any negative emotion. You are more powerful and energized when you are excellence-oriented. Besides, your inspiration is long-lasting.

When you are inspired by competition you are motivated by outside forces; in other words you are a slave and not an independent being. All these values are harmonizing values, as they would not, in normal circumstances, result in conflicts.

> All the values which are not conducive to growth or
> Are Against Harmony must be rejected.
>
> Self-centred value system vs. non-self-centred value system.
>
> Right-oriented value system vs. Duty-oriented value system.
>
> Selfishness motivated value system vs. *tyāga* oriented value system.

As can be seen from discussion so far, these values can be further expanded. A mere mention of some more values will suffice.

All the festivals can be looked at from this view. They help us grow and/or they help us to live in harmony.

Guiding Principles for Family

(1) From each as per his/her ability and to each as per his/her needs.

(2) *Aṅgāṅgī Bhāva*: That is treating the members of a family as if they are different organs of a body. If left hand is hurt right hand automatically massages the hand without thinking, why should it do that? Even again and again. This is how a family should behave in fulfilling needs of other members of the family.

(3) In a family the needs of the old, babies, sick, etc. are paramount and they should receive the maximum attention. Sometimes one sees the older folks, not complaining due to their self-respect, and do not ask

for help. This should be of extreme importance before the younger generation. One has to develop an attitude by extending imagination, as if entering their body in a hypothetical way to gain at least partial insight.

Conclusion

These principles are a guide. They optimize the aggregate total happiness of the whole family. They do not maximize the individual material benefits. They sure have a great potential in maximizing the individual happiness in the opinion of this writer, because one can also raise the standard of one's happiness to a broader perspective and find the individual happiness through the happiness of others within the family. If by following the rules of traffic we maximize safety at the cost of individual independence, we can also maximize the sum total of the average happiness of all the individuals of a family by following the values described and hinted in this essay. Looking from a higher angle they are also spiritually elevating.

References

Bleifeld, Maurice, *Biology and Evolution*, Barron's Educational Series.

Jhaveri, Madhusudan, various presentations at conferences organized by WAVES and Center for Indic Studies, and Newman Lecture Series at University of Massachusetts.

Krishna, Gopi, *The Biological Basis of Religion and Genius*, New York: NC Press, Inc.

Ramendra, *Dharma-Darśana*, Delhi: Motilal Banarsidass.

Upadhyay, D.D., *Integral Humanism*.

3

Joint Family System

C.M. Bhandari

As science and technology (S&T) seek to completely dominate our lives and the governing fundamentals transform into global standards, there is an accompanying yearning gaining ground for reflecting on the traditions and customs of the past, especially in the developed societies. This is because whereas the S&T have provided solutions by way of material comforts, they have also distanced people from time-tested human values. Many developmental activities are also in conflict with Nature's laws and are disturbing ecological balance besides creating irreversible pollutions by way of non-biodegradable products and damaging the environment. The common observation worldwide is that the more we move towards materialism, the more we get pushed towards individualism. Me and Mine become the primary concern even in holy alliances of parents and children or husband and wife. Everything else is secondary to the "I" and "Mine." This is why many in the West, notably from the Asian and African societies, are at crossroads, not knowing for sure which way to go — hang on to their own cultures and traditions, adopt the Western value systems or find a balance in between. This article seeks to look at the joint family system of yore in India and examines its relevance and practicality in the present times.

It also examines the changing social norms, value systems and human behaviour with time and place and looks at the role of religion in promoting human values and fellowship, a key ingredient in upholding the joint family norms. The author's own family tree will be used by way of a case study to illustrate the issues wherever so required.

Joint Family and Religion — Some Definitions

Let us first clarify the definition of a joint family. In the good old Vedic days, a joint family meant four generations living together. Even until half a century ago, it was not uncommon to find four generations living together happily and three generations living together was a common norm. At least one of the sons would take care of the ageing parents in case they were living separately for practical reasons like service, schooling, other compulsions, etc. In other words, they had strong bonds and attachment for each other. They would meet and visit each other very often if not living together. Presently, the family units in urban centres in India mostly comprise of parents and unmarried children living together under one roof whereas in rural India, the three to four generations still live together unless material well-being has changed the mindset and resulted in grown-up children charting their separate destinies. For the purposes of this discussion, the joint family seeks to combine grandparents also with the family unit of parents and children, in other words three generations living together or maintaining strong bonds of kinship.

In my family, my father had one sister and three brothers. They were born in the village and lived together until job search moved the brothers away and the sister went to her in-laws' after marriage. But the bonds were always maintained and they rushed to each other in their hours of joy or grief.

My grandparents shared their time between their children and ancestral home in the hills. We ourselves are six brothers and three sisters and my uncle has four daughters and one son. We never felt that we were cousins and freely lived with each other depending on educational or other requirements. My father's elder brother had passed away at a very young age leaving behind his young wife who had no child. She lived the rest of her nearly 75 years in the joint family and was always treated as the head of the joint family. All the nine sons and daughters of the two brothers from my father's side are now married and have children but we still continue to share our ancestral home and rush to each other in joys and sorrows, though most of us live separately in different cities or even countries. The family tree in the annexure will amply demonstrate this reality.

Let us also define religion at the outset by asking questions like: What is religion? What is its real purpose? How does it help, etc.? In Sanskrit, there is no equivalent word for religion. The closest is *dharma* but even *dharma* does not have a fixed meaning and can be given numerous interpretations depending on the context. Following two definitions of *dharma* illustrate the point:

> In the end, *dharma* provides the special rights and obligations, inter-personal relationships and the code of conduct for all human beings and is a symbol of the social order.
>
> — P.V. Kane

> All the good deeds that one can perform in life and the high moral standards observed in personal conduct, are included in *dharma* but there is no singular/specific feature/quality that defines *dharma*.
>
> — Chandra Kant Shukla

Religion thus is a "code of conduct," a "symbol of social order," "good deeds," "high moral standards," etc. which

Vaṁśāvali (Family Tree)

Present - Arjun Dev, the founder of our village Mawara or Mawada

Generation 1	Generation 2	Generation 3	Generation 4	Generation 5
Bhagi	Manorath	Jai Ram		
Ratan	Gautam	Baika		
		Padarath	Motiram	Jaidev, Devi Dutt, Rudra Dutt, Kamlapati, Chandra Mani*
			Ramapati	Dharmananda
			Kamlapati	Radha, Narottam, Shiv Dutt
			Jasa	Pandev, Baldev

* Chandramani Ji (generation 5) had four sons as the 6th generation — Hira Ballabh**

Jai Kishan (had no progeny), Keshav Dutt and Daya Ram.

Keshav Dutt	Ram Dutt	Munni Harish Pooran	Pushpa, Champa, Umesh, Rekha, Jagdish, Sanjay, Neeraj, Manju, Lalit, Kusum, Renu, Kavita, Shobha, Deep, Rashmi
Daya Ram	Narayan Dutt Amba Dutt Yamuna Dutt	Vinod Khazan	

** Children of Parent Hira Ballabh, wife Yashoda Devi (generation 6):

Generation 7	Generation 8	Generation 9
Anandi (Bua) h Narayan Datt Pant	Hansi h H.B. Joshi Madan w Medha Ganga h M.B. Tiwari	Devendra, Deepa, Yogendra Malvika, Suruchi, Sumati, Ashish Hem Chandra, Meeta, Anita
Hari Kishan, wife Lalita	(Tauji died soon after marriage). Jarja lived in the joint family as the family head after death of grandparents.	
Pitamber Datt (Babuji) wife Damiyanti (Iza)	Mahesh w Bharti Jagdish w Prabha Harish w Radha Girish w Hema Chander w Meena Ramesh w Ritu Nirmala h Prakash Manju h Hari Jyoti h Basant	Deepesh w Ami, Neetesh w Laxmi Pushpesh w Garima, Rachana h Anirudh, Anjana h Vance Ranjita, Kanak Abhishek, Manisha,Vidisha Aparita h Rajesh, Samahita, Jayant Raksha, Aman Pooja h Vikas, Arti h Sumit, Deepika, Bhavna, Rishabh Divya h Karan, Nakul Saumya, Siddharth
Laxmi Narayan wife Madhi (Chachaji & Chachiji)	Uma h Praful Ashu h Puran Sumita h Ajay Ramit w Bhawana Namita h Manoj	Ruchita, Deepika, Devaashish Neha, Samartha Avijit, Abhinit Anish Ishaan

Generation 10: Four sons and one daughter have so far been born in the tenth generation of males of our immediate family. Deepesh has Akshaya and Aashvi, Neetesh has Devang and Aditya, Pushpesh has Viraj, Rachana has Chaitra and Arti has Yash from the girls side.

all relate to an individual's personality. Religion therefore helps to shape one's personality in conformity with its teachings. It is a tool for character building, for imbibing high moral standards, which help to become a responsible member of the society. Religion is not an ideology that needs to be propagated by way of a political theory, identity or dogma. It is not surprising that all the religions of the world teach the same value systems even though their practices may be different, reflecting the physical and social realities of the times when they were first propounded by their respective founders. But the Vedas, from which the Vedic religion (now also understood as the Hindu religion) derives its practices, are said to be *apauruṣeya*, not authored by any particular prophet or religious leader. Likewise, the holy Qur'an was also revealed to Prophet Mohammed (Peace Be Upon Him). All other scriptural texts are narrations, commentaries or expositions by the prophets, religious masters and learned scholars based on their own realizations and experiences in life.

The present-day understanding of the word religion is best described by R.C. Majumdar, a historian of repute:

> Religion, in its essence, is based largely on intuition and emotion and not on a purely rational attitude of mind, and it is inspired and fed by faith and belief rather than reason and argument. While this offers no great difficulty in appreciating the essence of any particular religious belief, it is a standing obstacle to the historical interpretation of religion and its critical appraisal, which can only proceed on the basis of reason and reason alone.
>
> — *The Cultural Heritage of India*, vol. IV, p. 31, Ramakrishna Mission, Kolkata.

We also know that from time to time as people deviated from fundamental reason and truth of their religion beyond

6 - Honorable C.M. Bhandari, the then Indian ambassador to United Arab Emirates

6a - C.M. Bhandari, presenting his paper

tolerable limits, reformers were born to reset the balance. In India, the numerous religious leaders born over the past three millennia are a testimony to it and some of them became founders of new religions — Buddhism, Jainism and Sikhism — for their followers. Prophet Mohammed (PBUH) likewise had opposed idol worship/witchcraft and other maladies in the society to lay the foundation of Islam on the basis of revelations he received from Allāh.

In Sikhism, the directive of the tenth *guru* of the Sikhs, Guru Gobind Singhji Mahārāj, to do away with the succession of the *gurus* and instead make the teachings of the *gurus* enshrined in their holy book, the *Guru Granth Sahib* as their eternal *guru*, was a benchmark decision that clearly establishes the pre-eminence and permanence of the teachings, which are based on fundamental human values that are beyond the time, space or race variables. In present times when we are faced with daunting issues like ethnic, religious or cultural divide, the "clash of civilizations" debate, etc. there is need to rise above faith and belief issues and with an open mind, return to fundamentals, sound reasoning and convincing arguments. Only then can the dream of a peaceful and stable world order be realized. Without digressing any further, let me now return to the main thrust of this article, the joint family system, that to my mind is the basic unit for building a peaceful and caring world order.

In Thailand, the word for religion is *shaashanaa*, which is derived from the Sanskrit word *śāsana* or discipline. I think this is a very articulate word to describe the purpose of religion, which is to bring certain standards in personal, family and social codes of conduct.

Joint Family System: History

Two original works of yore from among a plethora of texts

for studying the history of the Indian social system are the *Manu-Smṛti* and the *Yājñavalkya-Smṛti*. As per the Indian scriptures and more specifically the *Śrīmadbhāgavat Mahāpurāṇa*, the human race is the progeny of Manu and Śatarūpā who were born when Lord Brahmā, the creator of this universe, was thinking about ways and means to multiply the human race when his body suddenly split into two parts, one male and the other female. They are said to be the first couple to have children by copulating. But it is not certain if the *Manu-Smṛti* text was actually authored by the same Manu. It is more likely that hundreds or thousands of generations later, some sage scripted the available Smṛtis or recollections that were being passed on from generation to generation by word of mouth, and named it *Manu-Smṛti* to commemorate the original proponent of the wisdom. *Manu-Smṛti* is regarded as the most detailed and ancient treatise on family structure and society in ancient India while *Yājñavalkya-Smṛti* provides further analysis of the subject. It may be of interest to many that the Vedas are not creations of some learned sage(s) but revelations by Lord Brahmā himself as he alone knew the whole truth about the universe and the human race. His sons and others listened to Vedic wisdom from him and therefore, they were called the Śrutis or audios.

The Smṛtis had provided a detailed social structure and code of conduct or *dharma* for propagation of the human race and orderly running of the society. The entire subject is divided into three parts, namely personal conduct (*ācāra*), social interaction (*vyavahāra*) and repentance (*prāyaścitta*, including undergoing austerities and even punishment for wrongdoings).

The basic objective of human birth was fourfold, *puruṣārtha catuṣṭaya*, namely *dharma, artha, kāma* and *mokṣa* or learning the righteous path of life and earning a righteous livelihood, producing children and seeking freedom from the cycle of birth and death, respectively.

The society was broadly divided into four groups, namely brāhmaṇas, kṣatriya, vaiśya and śūdra (the first three were also called as *dvija*), what in present-day parlance is known as the caste system. But in reality, this division was purely on the basis of each person's personal conduct and deeds. Birth in a particular family was not responsible for such a division. Even *Bhagavad-Gītā* very clearly brings out this fact in chapter IV, verse 13: *cāturvarṇyaṁ mayā sṛṣṭaṁ guṇākarma-vibhāgaśaḥ*" — "the four divisions are created by me on the basis of the individual's personal conduct and deeds." In Puruṣa-Sūkta from *Ṛgveda*, it is clearly mentioned that the mouth of the creator, Lord Brahmā, is the brāhmaṇa, his hands are the kṣatriya, his abdomen the vaiśya and his legs the śūdra. In other words, just as every part of the body has a specific role to perform, different people and society had different roles to play, which happens even now. We talk of gender equality, equal opportunity, etc. but that does not mean that everyone is doing the same work or receiving the same remuneration. It depends on the qualifications, capabilities, opportunities available, etc.

Further, the entire lifespan, which then averaged 100 years, was divided into four periods (*āśrama*s) of 25 years each, namely *brahmacarya, gṛhastha, vānaprastha* and *saṁnyāsa*. The first 25 years were spent in learning and gaining skills and knowledge depending on the individual's own capacity. The person observed strict celibacy and rigorous daily routine to acquire proficiency in the chosen vocation. Thereafter, the next 25 years were spent in earning a livelihood and leading a family life, giving birth and nursing children. The couple also took care of the elderly in the family. The next 25 years were spent in providing supervision to the family in the capacity of grandparents and the remaining 25 years were spent in seclusion in forests (in today's custom shifting to the old age homes but the real idea of *Saṁnyāsa* is total detachment from worldly affairs), trying to understand the mysteries of this life and working for deliverance from the cycle of birth and death.

It would be seen from the above that the period of 25 years in *gr̥hastha* is the most important part of every individual. In this, the *gr̥hasthī* (householder) not only looks after himself, he also takes care of the rest of the family in the other three *āśrama*s, more notably of those in *brahmacarya* and *vānaprastha* as the members in these two categories are mostly dependent on him for their day-to-day well-being.

I had occasion to attend to my octogenarian mother who had become bedridden due to normal degeneration of brain from old age. Her memory was fading. Her behaviour towards the last year of her life (2005) was no different from an infant's. In fact, the response of we nine adult children of hers towards her was no different from that towards our own children when they were infants. We treated her just like a few months old baby, caressing her with all the fondness and love. For the first time I got the true realization of what has been provided in the Smr̥tis. Therefore, of all the four periods in one's entire life cycle, the most important *āśrama* is *gr̥hastha* and this is the reason that all Smr̥tis mostly deal with the institution of marriage and the rights and responsibilities of husband and wife towards each other, as also towards all the family members — children, parents, grandparents and great-grandparents.

In this connection, it is also important to note that four generations had generally coexisted until half a century ago. In our family, my mother was witness to three great-grandsons being born from her sons' side. This fact is also corroborated from memorial services in Indian traditions, which are offered up to three generations by name for the departed married male members and their wives if deceased, both from husband and wife's families. This ritual of offering food and water to ancestors is observed even in several countries of South-East and East Asia. I am reminded of the Aboriginals in Australia and Red Indians in the American continent who also have elaborate rituals for their ancestors.

Having thus argued of the existence of a sound family structure and relationships from the very beginning of the human race, a passing reference may be made to the large numbers of ancient Indian texts, like the Vedas, the Purāṇas, the Upaniṣads, the two well-known epics — *Rāmāyaṇa* and *Mahābhārata*, and recorded history of India since the Indus Valley Civilization to state that the joint family tradition has continued to sustain societies since time immemorial. Other civilizations also, even if they did not have any such elaborate codification of the joint family structure as the Smṛtis in India, have lived in the family structure since time immemorial. It is also true that wars have been fought for supremacy, sometimes within families, since as far back as the evolution of human civilization and continue even now. With growing sizes of political entities, geographical areas occupied and populations living within them, the wars also became that much more violent and far-reaching in affecting the lives of the ordinary people. The economic and social inequalities in the world that we see today are ongoing phenomena and despite well-intentioned initiatives for a just and sustainable world economic and social order, the situation appears to be moving from bad to worse.

If the institution of joint family has come under intense strain in our times, it is not difficult to visualize why. The materialism of today did not exist in the past. If I look back just 50 years when I went to school, there were no computers, no television, no population pressure or other distractions and the three main requirements for living were food, clothing and shelter. Giving children birth, having large families and creating wealth determined the prosperity of a family. Living together was the main assurance for social security, and Nature's law of survival of the fittest ruled supreme. With passage of time everything in the universe has been evolving though there are certain fundamentals that remain constant like the five basic elements — sound, air, water, fire and earth — and laws of Nature. But beyond that the human intelligence and desire, the two main motive forces for all developments and changes, have been responsible to bring us to the point where science and technology are the driving forces of a globalizing economy but a divided society. If economic forces are against political borders, nationalistic forces regiment against it, at least that has been the experience until now.

Case Studies

If the joint family system survived in the past and flourishes in developing rural societies even now, it is because it provides the fundamental social security mechanism to everyone living within it. Everyone in the joint family abides by a given code of conduct and shares responsibility. The Smṛtis had codified the rights and responsibilities of every member of the family, which was called *dharma* and developed on certain moral principles, which reflected Nature's laws and were to everyone's advantage. If we see a certain dilution in the strict compliance of that code of conduct in the present times, it is because of the fact that the state has taken over that authority, the same is being legislated under national constitutions and administered by the respective governments of the day. In developed countries, the state provides for social security in return for the taxes. But in olden times, the family structure provided social security, which is still the norm in many countries, including India. The state ensured that the rule of *dharma* prevailed and even the ruler was not above it. We hear of King Janaka in the epic *Rāmāyaṇa* who lived the life of a renunciate and used to tour his kingdom during night as a commoner to see for himself if his administration was just and served the people. King was the embodiment of God and acknowledged his divine responsibility of ensuring the welfare of his subject.

I had the opportunity to serve in Cambodia as Ambassador of India to that country where the tradition of God kings is still reflected in the ninth-to-fifteenth centuries Angkor temples. In Thailand, the constitutional monarch, King Bhumibol Adulyadej, also called Phra Rama IX in the succession of kings of the Rāma dynasty, is still revered by the Thai people as the embodiment of God and literally worshipped with godly reverence. In Nepal, the ruling Shah dynasty was seen to be the incarnation of Lord Viṣṇu until the parliament passed the resolution on 18 May 2006 to do away with the title of "His Majesty" because of the misadventures of the then king who did not distinguish himself in that role of a God king. In all tribal societies across the globe where the modern society has yet to make inroads, the family structures are strong. We still talk of Asian value systems, which place high priority on family unit. In Africa also, the family unit is intact. In fact, during my stay in Lagos, Nigeria between 1982-84, I used to hear the phrase "My brother (or my sister) — same father same mother." This was to indicate blood relation as otherwise everyone coming from the village was a brother, sister, uncle or aunt — and was given the due attention, including paying for his or her return to the village. I had not understood the significance of this relationship until recently when I got the family tree of our own village and learnt that all the families numbering over 500 or more now from our village, are indeed cousins spread over 11 generations.

The first four generations had one, two, three and four family heads respectively. Thereafter, the fifth generation had 10 family heads, the sixth had 27, the seventh 64, the eighth 144, the ninth 170 and the tenth 57. Only male children are counted for family tree though many daughters were also born and married outside the village. I belong to the eighth generation. My father had seven sons and three daughters. Except for the seventh son who died of drowning when he was still under five years, all others are doing well in their respective places and some are blessed with grandchildren. Our father passed away in 2001 at the ripe age of 87 years and mother in 2005 in her mid-eighties. My older uncle died soon after marriage in 1936 but his wife lived as a childless widow in our joint family with full honours until her death in 2001. My younger uncle and aunt have left behind one son and four daughters. I am happy to say that we still have very close ties between the children of the last four generations of ours, starting with our grandfather. The fifth generation is now in the making and four sons have been born so far.

But come to think of our entire village, we are all related, a fact which was not so clear to me except the fact that in our village, we all are Bhandaris except for three or four families. I also now realize why the individual landholdings in our village are so tiny. Our forefather Shri Arjun Dev had perhaps come to the hill slope of our village and found enough fertile land and water to make a living. But as the family tree started growing and could not stay in the joint family structure beyond two-three generations, the land holding kept getting divided generation after generation, resulting in decreasing sizes of landholdings with every division. This fact makes it absolutely clear that the extended family could not stay as one unit for all times in one place and needed new pastures. This has to be acknowledged as the law of Nature. Even the corporate world has not been spared from it. When your business expands, you decide to float a new company at the appropriate time for better management. But the basic unit of three generations has normally lived as one entity to begin with and divided when the numbers became too large to manage or when the family heads could not have unity of opinions. The best example is of the Ambani brothers of the Reliance group in India who honourably decided to part ways in 2005 by dividing their father's corporate empire of billions of dollar and both new corporate groups are now breaking new grounds and reaching greater heights.

Returning to my own village, the reducing size of land-holdings and inability to make both ends meet led people from sixth generation onwards to move out to nearby towns for middle (eighth grade) or high school level education, which helped them to get government jobs, which in turn catapulted some of them to bigger cities and towns. They provided helping hands to their siblings and thus the journey of outward migration started in the 1930s and today, our village is begging for people to come back. The old majestic dwelling houses in stone with highly carved wooden doors and windows and other antiquities are now mostly desolated, eaten away by termites and collapsed. But the overcrowding in urban cities and pollution levels are now driving people back to Nature and some of us are craving to return to our village by providing modern facilities to turn it into a more liveable place. The scarcity of water however has become a real issue in the Himalayan region with depleting glaciers and disappearing vegetative cover.

When I read about the family tree of the eleven generations of Bhandari family, I also learnt that there were intense family disputes after fifth generation for distribution of paternal landholdings because of survival issues and each brother had tried to grab as much land as possible, which in some cases led to civil litigation also among the cousins. But today when our village presents a deserted look, several of them from different branches of the last four generations of ours are trying to form a co-operative to be able to put our miniscule landholdings together to form an economy of scale. We are trying to engage the whole village as one unit and carry some common economic activities that will allow some profits to be generated and employment created. This situation has arisen because most of us have our main economic activities elsewhere and the village project is primarily to see that our ancestral land and property is not ruined and our ancestors would be pleased to see that we have tried to revive the old richness of the place that attracted our forefather to settle in that picturesque hill some 150 years ago when the only means of transport to those remote hills was on-foot or by domestic animals.

When I look at my own joint family of nine surviving brothers and sisters, I feel humbled that we have maintained certain value systems. But the credit for this has to go to our parents' generation who provided us a disciplined upbringing and empowered us with a lot of human value systems in the early years of our life. My father had humble beginnings. After finishing his eighth class in the village, he came to Mussoorie in 1934 where his brother-in-law (elder sister's husband) helped him get a paramedic apprenticeship in the hospital. He later completed a nine-month pharmacy course in Meerut and by 1937, got a regular job of a Pharmacist in the Prince of Wales School Hospital, Dehra Dun. He got married the same year and the responsibility to support and educate nine of his own children besides cousins over the next 30 years, was no easy task for our parents. So, they both worked very hard and besides the salary from my father's work, both of them supplemented the family income by cultivating land and rearing cattle for selling milk.

As the number of children increased, he bought wasteland in instalments, which was then available at throwaway prices but still difficult for him to buy in one go from his petty savings. He made all of us spend our free time in tilling the soil and producing foodgrains for our own consumption. The agriculture and dairy activities also complemented and supplemented each other. In hindsight, those were the most precious days of our life, which taught us the dignity of manual labour and also kept us away from normal teenage distractions. I can say with a lot of confidence that many of the difficulties of the present-day society are because of material prosperity and move towards individualism. There is not much time for caring and sharing between the family members. Everything appears to be contract-oriented. Even marriage, the most sacred of relationships, is a contract in modern legal language. In the Smr̥tis, the institution of marriage is sacrosanct, solemnized only once for the whole lifetime but now one can marry and seek divorce as soon as the law of the land permits.

When my father got settled in Dehra Dun in 1937, he had to take care of his younger brother and sister's son's education. They lived with him. Then my mother's brother also came and lived with them for education for some time. This tradition continues and all of us treat it as a matter of right to be with our first cousins without any hesitation. I had seven years of education at different times by living with my uncle. My younger brother and two sisters also lived with uncle for education. Uncle's daughter lived with me for two years in Delhi to do her Masters degree. My second brother who is now an American citizen, has helped so many of the family members for their higher education in the US, and so on. But I must qualify that a family has two pillars — the husband and the wife — and both have to be like-minded to move this institution of joint family together. This is where we find that if sufficient compatibility is not ascertained before marriage and after marriage, great sacrifices are not made by way of adjustments and understandings, it does not take long for things to turn sour. Therefore, the joint family system can thrive only if all the members are committed to some basic moral principles and are prepared for sacrifices and adjustments to promote family unity and harmony.

Pros and Cons

Be that as it may, we may now examine the pros and cons of the joint family system. The pressures of urban living are driving people to nuclear families comprising of the married couple and their unmarried children. In rural India, it is still common to see three generations coexisting, living in the same home. In cities, the grandparents visit their children from time to time for short durations. It is not uncommon even in cities to find well-disposed children and their spouses ensuring that the parents are not abandoned in their hour of need. In the case of we nine members, we all had moved out from our parents' home because of our vocations and therefore, there was no joint living, specially after marriage, for long periods of time. We all came home for festivals, other family celebrations like marriages or more solemn occasions like death, and were overjoyed to see all of us cherish our parents' sacrifices in bringing us up to be highly educated and at the same time, providing us such noble thoughts of togetherness. The bond between us has been as before and each one of us wanted to care for our parents, more than the others, till their very last.

Also, everyone had materially enough of one's own and no one looked for a share in the common parental property. If at all, the problem is who will look after the ancestral land? So, one cardinal principle for promoting joint family norm is threadbare — humble beginnings that ignite the instinct for survival and seek adjustment in every situation. On the other hand, too much wealth and lavish lifestyles are the beginnings of diseases, disputes and division. We are aware of the many property disputes in recent decades in the corporate world globally and more specifically in India. As already referred in case of the Ambani brothers, both Mukesh and Anil showed great maturity and thanks to the mentoring of their parents who too had very humble beginnings, theirs is a very good example of how transparency in sharing wealth and property matters can help carry forward the joint family values and norms.

The Scenario for Our Coming Generations: Arranged vs. Love Marriages

Arrival of a new bride in the family is a time of celebrations but it also heralds the start of a process of major adjustments for all the family members. There has to be good understanding and effort on the part of everyone in the family and the newly arrived bride to ensure love and harmony all around. There is no guarantee that an arranged marriage has a better rate of success than a love marriage because marriage is not just a relationship between the married couple but much more. Every marriage has three balancing factors to be looked at and unless all three are taken good care of, adjustment problems in the joint family norm cannot be ruled out. The three aspects relate to: (i) the compatibility of the couple between themselves, (ii) between the two families from the boy and girl's side being united in wedlock, and (iii) acceptance of the marriage by the society. All three aspects are equally important and cannot be ignored in the longer-term perspective.

I have been witness to situations where our children have forced their ways into marriages after years of courtship and then walked out of them much faster. The reality unfortunately dawns when it is too late that it is not the same thing before marriage and after marriage and sacrifices and adjustments are called for from both the bride and groom in the first place, leave aside the family and society compatibilities. Everything changes, right from feelings and behaviour of the couple towards each other to responses from family members, and the society before and after marriage. Before marriage, everyone allows a lot of flexibility and room, hoping that things will fall in place and the other side will adjust. After marriage, everyone wants the other one to change and not self and that's where things start falling apart. Minor irritants become major, positions start hardening and slight provocation from one side results in matching or even more severe response from the other side, leading finally to the break up and divorce as the path of least resistance.

I am reminded of my own search for a bride when a friend of mine took me to the house of his friend who had a marriageable daughter. He thought that she would be a good match for me and that her father would be most gratified to know about me and my position in career. To our amazement, nothing like that happened. He gave us full respect and hospitality but despite my friend's repeated introduction of me and the purpose of our visiting him, he did not want to talk about the marriage prospect as he did not think it was proper for him to introduce his daughter at the first step. When my friend finally pressed him for at least calling the girl to meet us, he told us that unless he has first examined the compatibility of the proposed relationship from the society and family angles, he did not think the personal compatibility of the two of us had any meaning. He thought that was the last thing to be looked at.

In fact, in our community until about two decades back, the first starting-point for seeking a marriage alliance used to be compatibility of the two lineages from which the boy and the girl hail. If that was found appropriate and also the family status of the two parties was compatible, then the horoscopes would be looked at by the boy's side, for the bride moves to the boy's home and it was primarily for them to ensure that the bride will become a happy addition to their family. Only after the horoscopes confirmed the like-mindedness of the two that they would then discuss the possible alliance between the two families and only thereafter, if at all, would they allow the boy and the girl to meet for their consent. There was no courtship. Just half a century ago, the boy and the girl never met each other and their parents took the final decision on their own. Marriage was a very auspicious union said to be made in heaven and once solemnized, the two had to make it a success. There was no path of least resistance like the divorce.

Talking of horoscopes, the thought comes to my mind whether it has any relevance today. My nephew who now lives in New York and married to an Indian American Gujarati girl, was blessed with their second child last month.

They knew in advance of the sex of the child and had given her a name also. The parents had decided the approximate day of birth to suit the presence of grandma from India. Many parents now plan for their child to be the first to be born on Christmas day or New Year day. I remember when my third child was to be born, the doctor had told us that if the delivery did not take place by a given date, she would induce the delivery. In other words, one can even determine the date and approximate time of birth of the child. Now because the horoscope is dependent on three variables, namely date, time and place of birth, all three of which can easily be predetermined by the parents, it should then imply that the parents can predetermine the destiny of the child. This just illustrates the point of the extent to which human factor is now determining the course of events on the earth and not divine bodings alone. If that be so, do issues like the joint family system, horoscopes, etc. have any relevance? I still think that past traditions do have relevance though these would need to be understood in proper perspective and not just by way of blind faith. I know first-hand in my daughter's case where the horoscopes of her and the boy she wanted to marry did not click and the priest was dead against the wedding but we still went ahead with the wedding. To our shock, the horoscope predictions proved true.

I have nothing against the arranged marriage system. All parents want their children to be happy and prosperous and would do their best to find them the most deserving match. Also, there is no denying that the parents are better placed to weigh the pros and cons of a marriage alliance, for they have their own marriage experience of over 25 years or so and precisely know what ultimately matters in life. The young minds are mostly driven by sense impulses, which do not last. I remember my mother telling us that the concept of beauty is short-lived as, after marriage, even an ugly spouse appears beautiful/handsome, for beauty lies in the eyes of the beholder. The parents make detailed enquiries about the prospective bride or groom, the family, and also consult other relatives. But it is also true that in the present age of science and technology, the prospective couple must also get sufficient opportunity to know each other and approve of their getting united in wedlock. This balance will definitely ensure a better success rate of the marriages.

I also have nothing against love marriages where the men and women make their own choices without necessarily receiving approval of their respective families. For one, they are educated, worldly wise, generally have been economically independent and gained maturity in running a household. What they do lack are the complexities and intricacies of a marital union. No amount of reading or knowing from others' experiences is going to give a clear understanding of the real issues after marriage unless the two individuals are not obligated at all to their respective families and/or communities. It is really extraordinary that the same two persons should look at each other quite differently after marriage. I have seen in our community and society children claiming to know their future better than their parents and insisting that they were doing the right things. But it did not take even a year in some cases to realize that they were not right. Unfortunately such cases are not few to be forgotten as exceptions. The glitter and impulse of senses indeed makes us blind, and also perverts our intellect, so that we are unable to take the right decisions. I would therefore recommend that while we do encourage them to court but this should be after the initial compatibilities have been looked at. Also, they have to be told of some basic minimum understandings about life after marriage that they must evaluate before deciding to get married. The two families' approval would definitely make the wedding that much more happy, stronger and with better chances of success.

Another very important factor to be appreciated is the concept of "conflict of interest." In legal parlance, a judge cannot preside on his own case, that is if he/she is a party to the dispute or has a conflict of interest in the case. Likewise, deciding on your own marriage partner is a delicate issue since there is a conflict of interest, you yourself being a party to it. The other day, I was debating on this issue in my mind when I came up with another example, that of being unable to see ourselves. Come to think of it, none of us can see our own face unless we look into a mirror or a reflecting surface. So, to see our own features, we need a mirror. Seeing the inner self is even more complicated, for it can be camouflaged by our sense impulses and intellect. We visit the temple, the mosque, the church, the *gurdwārā* or a *pagoḍā* to reflect on our inner self. So, we do need an external medium to help us see our own face, our own inner self. Then why should there be any hesitation in consulting your family and friends about someone you want to be your lifelong partner? Certainly have your say about it but do leave the final decision to someone more impartial.

Broken Families

It is not uncommon now to find single parents having to struggle and seek compromise. The children born to them are the worst sufferers. Any misunderstanding between the parents casts a dark shadow on the minds of the children, especially if they are in their teens or under and even if they have no clear understanding of the whole issue. If the couple is at loggerheads and out to take revenge on one another, then the children are the worst sufferers and their own adulthood and career prospects get seriously affected. By comparison, families where parents have complete understanding about responsibility of each one of them towards the joint family, they are able to manage everything well even with humble resources and their children turn out to be better citizens. I am of the firm belief that children must be given a gentle handling but a disciplined upbringing, so that they understand the dignity of labour and eternity of human values. They must be well educated but at the same time, well mannered and understand social obligations in life. Individuality has to move hand in hand with team spirit. Self should dominate until the basic minimum survival is not assured but beyond that, greed should not lead to exploitation of others. We have to always remember that we do not do to others what we will not like others to do to us. Every religion teaches this kind of eternal truths and we should be open to such teachings no matter from which religion or land it comes from. As the *R̥gveda* saying goes: *ā no bhadrā kratvoyantu viśvataḥ*, meaning let noble thoughts flow in from all over.

Individuals together make families. The structure of the family will be dependent on each member of the family. Just as the strength of a chain lies in its weakest link, the weaker members of the family need that much more understanding from other members. The family head has to be more tolerant than the spouse, the parents have to be more tolerant than the children, the elder of the siblings will have to be more tolerant of the youngsters. Only when there is this degree of understanding and help from one another that the success of a joint family or for that matter, any society can never be in doubt. It is when a member in the family wants to take care of only oneself that problems start and then it does not take long for even the best-knit families to fall apart.

I am reminded of Mother Teresa when she had arrived in Oslo on 10 December 1979 to receive her Nobel Peace Prize and was asked at the airport press conference: "You have been working with the destitutes of Kolkata but what about the millions in the rest of the world?" Her response was very simple: "I have only two eyes and I can see only that far. I cannot worry for what I have not seen." In her Reply Speech after receiving the award, she had told the audience of the poverty of the developed world. She told them to go to their old age homes and see how poor their aged feel who are longing not for material gains but emotional comforts, some loved one visiting them and talking to them, comforting them for a while. This was the beauty of the joint family system where the grandparents had the divine company of innocent toddlers with whom they not only got regular exercises but also shared great moments. The children in return got exceptional care, general knowledge, human values and selfless love. This was a win-win tradition, which has come under severe strain due to the disappearing of time-tested social norms and value systems. The Western societies are now governed by lawyers and without their advice, you will be ill-advised to take even a small step in life.

Today, people rush to police, lawyers and counsellors for help to sort out their personal disputes and differences. In the past, the good old joint family system took care of such matters. It provided an in-house mechanism to air their pent-up emotions, give counselling, pull up or punish the erring member where and whenever necessary and comfort the ones wronged. Most issues were settled within the family members even though serious issues arose all the time, leading to differences and even fights. But when things went beyond repair or the numbers became too many, they did not hesitate to part ways and form new smaller establishments. Even Nature provides for expansion and multiplication of living beings. Indian scriptures, notably the *Mahābhārata* and *Rāmāyaṇa* are replete with interesting stories that help us learn the realities of life and benefit from them in our own daily living. If we cannot agree, at least we should be civilized enough to agree to disagree and carry on with our respective lives in our own ways. There is no point in allowing our differences to transform into animosities and violence — not afraid to even kill. The untimely and tragic death of Pramod Mahajan in Mumbai illustrates the point and reminds us that materialism should not enslave human values.

Conclusion

The four fundamental freedoms — freedom of expression, freedom of worship, freedom from want and freedom from fear — constitute the bedrock of democracy. In fact, all creatures look for these freedoms for their survival and perhaps constitute the *raison d'être* of the joint family institution. Even living plants have such affinities. All living creatures tend their newly borns. Even animals have family norms though they vary from specie to specie — some having strong family herds like the elephants while others parting ways as soon as the new-borns are on their feet or wings. I have seen dogs getting very attached to their keepers and celebrate or grieve with them to the extent of not eating food, caressing the grieving keeper, etc. or dancing in celebration. Such responses are dependent on the intelligence and memory development in each animal specie and capabilities of each individual animal.

It is therefore but natural that human beings should have a highly developed institution of joint family system since time immemorial and if it is breaking down in present times, it is primarily because of the temptations for a better fortune, though one cannot say for better life. If more and more people are finding solace in ancient practices like Yoga, Āyurveda, and simple lifestyles, it is primarily because materialism creates more desire and concomitantly more stress and unhappiness. Real happiness lies in contentment, being able to be of service to others/donate to others, which are also the founding principles of the joint family system. What needs to be particularly appreciated is that joint family does not mean that all should be living under one roof even if they are not on talking terms. It implies that they recognize and respect the kinship bonds between them and are there to rush to support each other in times of need. A happy joint family is the starting block for a happy society and that in turn can assure a happy global village.

4

Changing Contours of the Indian Family System
Its Impact on the Society

V.T. Patil

THE purpose of this essay is to specify and examine the main features of the Indian family system and to identify the enormous changes it has witnessed in recent years. In consonance with this objective the first part of the essay will briefly summarize the structure, practices, values and beliefs in the traditional joint family system. The second part will examine the impact of the transformation of the joint family system into the nuclear family or the post-nuclear family.

The following hypotheses will constitute the conceptual framework for analysis of the Indian family system:

- A nation in the process of transition from tradition to modernity undergoes changes in values, beliefs, practices and institutions.
- The joint family system which has established its resilience over a long period in Indian history may undergo a major transformation in the light of momentous systemic developments like the impact of modernization, globalization, liberalization and science and technology.

- The economic growth of nations oriented towards development of a material civilization in tandem with the communication revolution has enhanced mobility in human societies. These developments in turn may lead to the complete break-up of the Indian joint family into a nuclear family or post-nuclear family system.
- The joint family system — the basic socialization unit — as it gets transformed may trigger social crises leading to endemic violence and undermining of established institutions in the society.

India is a vast country of subcontinental proportions where people belonging to different castes, creeds, communities, languages, customs, and mores reside and mingle and intermingle with each other. The basic tenets of Indian cultural values/themes are practised and evolved within the family system. In other words, the Indian family is a basic unit of socialization for all its members. In this meaningful sense, the family constitutes one of the basic units of the Indian society. The most widely prevalent structural family unit is the patrilineal joint family. Karve very succinctly defines the joint family as "a group of people who generally live under one roof, who eat food cooked at one hearth, who hold property in common, who participate in common family worship, and who are related to each other as some particular type of kindred."[1] Living together in patrilocal residence members co-operate and share social, economic and cultural activities for mutual benefit. Further, in this set-up grandfathers, grandmothers, husbands, wives, sons, and daughters share a common roof, bondage and values.

---

1. I. Karve, *Kinship Organization in India*, Bombay: Asia Publishing House, 1965, p. 8.

The joint family system is ancient in origin and unique to India in terms of its nature, scope and significance. Historically, the joint family emphasizes a large family household and is well suited to the majority of India's population living in rural areas.[2] Agriculture being a major occupation for the bulk of the population, the joint family system helps individual members to secure gainful employment in agriculture-related activities. In a predominantly agricultural society, the joint family system ensures economic security to all the members of the family. This self-reliant and self-sustaining nature of the joint family system explains its resilience over a long period in India's history. The joint family system is also found in urban areas (though it has been declining rapidly in the last three decades), where interlocking relationships between kinship groups provide a major source and anchor for economic security.

The traditional joint family is made up of husband, wife, children, and grandparents. Usually the male member of the family lives with his parents and he has to look after them. His wife looks after the husband's parents as her parents. The male member has the onerous task of harmonizing relations between all members of the family. He has to keep his parents and wife satisfied and resolve any conflict between them. His wife as the daughter-in-law is often looked upon as a homemaker in the sense that she cooks for the family and takes care of her parents-in-law. After children are born she is expected to concentrate

2. The pattern of joint family households in rural areas in the historical past was similar in India and western Europe, vide "Family and Kinship in Western Europe: The Problem of the Joint Family Household", Robert Wheaton, *Journal of Interdisciplinary History*, vol. 5, no. 4, *The History of the Family*, II (Spring 1975), pp. 601-28.

completely on bringing up the children in terms of family norms. As this is the common practice in the traditional joint family, the husband as the principal earning member is expected to provide resources for the upkeep of the entire family. Arrangement of marriage of children when they grow up is a familial responsibility; the essence of this system is co-operation, stability and progress. From a historical perspective, traditional joint family values, practices and systems of family life have largely remained similar in most parts of India.

The core or essential elements of joint family system can be summed up as follows:

(a) Identity and recognition of joint family as a social unit in the caste and community in an essentially patriarchal society.

(b) Marriage regarded as sacrosanct and part of religious and social duty.

(c) Caste endogamy — an intrinsic part of joint family system.

(d) Domination of parent-child relations (Western tradition — domination of spousal relations in conjugal family).

(e) Familial responsibility for survival, socialization and eventually marriage of children as and when they grow up.

(f) Joint family provided the basis of economic security for its members.

(g) Common ownership of property.

The Indian experience with the joint family system has its own merits and defects. It is a common occurrence where parents-in-law and daughters-in-law do not get along with each other. This friction within the family vitiates the atmosphere and sometimes leads to its split. Generally, elder males in the family through tact and skill born out of experience cool down the pent-up emotions, repair bruised egos and provide equitable solutions to extant problems. In terms of the merit of the joint system, it provides an excellent opportunity for the children to learn a great deal from their grandparents. Additionally, the children have an opportunity to mingle with other children of their own age sharing the joy of playing together. The joint family ensures protection, adequate education and stable growth for children. All in all, the joint family system was taken very seriously in India and more often in the past has ensured economic security and progress of the family as a whole. Clearly, it has been a basic social unit of Indian society for a long period in its history, playing a functional and stabilizing role.

However, any social unit in the long run has to undergo transformation, sometimes little or sometimes more. Often values, practices, customs and beliefs change in consonance with changes in the environment — industrialization, modernization and globalization. The essential or core aspects of Indian joint family system presented in the earlier part of the essay have either got diluted or withered away or have lost their relevance under the impact of domestic and systemic forces.

The second and the important part of this essay will raise a number of pertinent questions on the transformation process. Which values, practices, traditions of the joint family have changed to keep in tune with socio-economic and political transformation and with what impact? Is the patriarchical element undergoing any change for the better or for the worse? What is the impact of changes in the joint family system on the status and position of women? What is the impact of reservation for weaker sections on Indian family? Can ritualism be a substitute for the real spirit of Indian society, culture and civilization? Can the joint family adequately address the role of humanism and scientific rationality? What is the impact of changes in joint family system on the growth of children? Is it possible to redefine the Indian joint family in the light of new responsibilities and new realities? What is the future of the joint family system in the third millennium? Is the joint family moving towards the nuclear family or into the phase of post-nuclear family? Hopefully, the rest of the essay will examine critically the significance, impact and consequences of the extent paradigmatic changes in the family system in an emergent India.

Indian society is at crossroads today. Under the impact of globalization[3] and modernization India has undergone major transformation in social, economic, cultural and other factors. Since the beginning of the liberalization process in 1991, the Indian economy has witnessed major upward movement in terms of economic development. India is among the fastest growing economies in the world with an annual rate of 7-9 per cent. The quantum leap into the future has led to the opening up of the Indian economy fuelled by massive domestic and foreign investments. While all these transformative changes have led to rapid economic growth, the impact on social, economic and political institutions is of a far-reaching nature. The existing scenario in India is

3. Globalization is not an unmixed blessing. As far as India is concerned, globalization has hastened the economic growth, but yet it is not sufficient in itself to solve massive problems of poverty and unemployment. Its impact on Indian society and culture is uneven in import and significance. In any case, globalization is not a magic wand or an Aladdin's lamp which can solve the complex problems of human society at one move.

such that the individual is pitted against groups, groups against the nation, and the nation against the Indian state. There is a crisis of national character/identity in a situation where centrifugal and centripetal forces compete with each other. The relationship between the centre and the periphery is neither solid nor co-operative. Many a time the centre (federal government) and the states do not see eye to eye on problems of national importance, and relations can at best be described as competitive/conflictive rather than co-operative. The emergence of a coalition culture of politics has added a new dimension to the multifarious problems of the Indian state. The assumption underlying the not too optimistic prognosis of the situation in India (though economic development is faster) in my opinion can be directly traced to the gradual break-up/disintegration of the traditional joint family system. Scholars discuss this change in terms of nuclear/conjugal family, the extended family, adaptive extended family, single parent family, dual earner family, etc. However, one common assumption in the literature on family is that major transformation in the joint family system is a persistent reality in India today.[4]

The joint family system traditionally sustained and developed the basic values of Indian culture and civilization for a long period in its chequered history. It was a primordial socialization force for all those who belonged to its fold, inculcating appropriate norms, values, beliefs, and practices

4. William J. Goode, *World Revolutions and Family Patterns*, New York: The Free Press of Glencoe, 1963. Also see George H. Conklin, "The Extended Family as an Independent Factor in Social Change: A Case of India", *Journal of Marriage and Family*, vol. 36, no. 4 (November, 1974), pp. 798-804; A.A. Khatri, "The Adaptive Extended Family in India Today", *Journal of Marriage and Family*, vol. 37, no. 3 (August, 1975), pp. 633-42.

into the system. It played a significant role in developing a strong cohesive and stable society. In the backdrop of the well-established joint family system, individual members of the family found ample scope for fructification of their hopes and aspirations for a better life for themselves and for others in the society. However, the big picture has changed and the joint family system no longer provides the platform and anchor for development of a stable and harmonious society. Old values, norms, beliefs, and practices like respect for authority and elders are rapidly withering away, hastening the breakdown of the traditional joint family system. Enormous changes have taken place in the post-liberalization period (1991) of the Indian economy. India has opened up many important sectors of the economy for massive domestic and foreign investment. The resultant economic growth has created enormous job opportunities in major sectors like Information Technology (IT), banking and other services, commerce and industrial sector. Even then millions of youth are still not able to get gainful employment. The post-Nehruvian generation and post-economic liberalization era (after 1991) have generated new pulls and pressures, and new issues and problems on the national scene.

The first major development in the post-Nehruvian period is the phenomenon of political violence where violence on a recurring scale is used for political purposes. Simultaneously, the authority structure of the elders in the joint family has declined *vis-à-vis* the younger members. The younger members yearn for more space and freedom to live their own lives the way they want. The generation gap between the elders and the younger members has whittled away the respect and obedience the former used to command from the latter. This has harmed the socialization process of the youth and they are left virtually to grope in the dark or to fend for themselves. Such a wide gap in their lives provides a fertile ground for them to indulge in activities which are contrary to the interest of the society. The youth have taken to violence in large numbers as is evident from their participation in Naxalite and Maoists organizations. Large parts of Bihar, some parts of Uttar Pradesh, Andhra Pradesh, Orissa, West Bengal, Chhattisgarh and north-eastern states are in the grip of resurgent violence. The ultra-left movements have taken advantage of massive rural unemployment which has created economic depression and frustration among the rural youth. It is a matter of great concern that these ultra-left movements are gaining strength by recruiting alienated youth to their movement. The emergence of Naxalite and Maoist movements in different parts of the country are ominous new developments where violence subserves ideological and political purposes. These fringe movements have the avowed objective to destabilize and undermine the authority of the Indian state.

In the past, the joint family — as the primary unit of socialization — provided the youth a sense of security and confidence. They were taught and they learnt the values of tolerance, compassion, forbearance and respect for elders/ authority. Now, in the absence of that platform/forum the rural/urban youth have become helpless, rudderless and rootless wanderers in search of jobs. The reality is that too many chase too few jobs. A sense of ennui, anomie and alienation is part of their life. It is not surprising to note that significant numbers have taken to consumption of alcohol and harmful drugs. The root of the problem lies in the emasculated joint family which has lost its élan and vitality. On the other hand, the Indian state is not able to accommodate the pent-up demands and soaring ambitions of youth. Given this situation, "revolution of rising expectations" of the youth degenerates into "revolution of rising frustrations."

Federal and state governments, non-governmental organizations (NGOs) and public spirited individuals must take immediate corrective measures to retrieve the situation. This would involve taking a close look at the present status of the Indian family. In a few years the youth would constitute 25 per cent of India's population — the largest in the world. No society and nation can become a major engine of growth when the most productive component of the population gets alienated from the mainstream of the society. Therefore, the first step should be to tackle the alarming development on a priority basis by taking a close look at the problems and issues of the Indian family system.

The rise of terrorism in Jammu & Kashmir is the result of cross-border terrorism by Pakistan, but is also due to the breakdown of the joint family system. The classic example is the total dislocation/breakdown and migration of the *paṇḍit* joint families from Jammu & Kashmir to other parts of the country. The traditional *paṇḍit* families played a very useful and stabilizing role in the state of Jammu & Kashmir.[5] The decline of the joint family system throughout the country is replicated in Jammu & Kashmir also. This explains why Muslim youths join terrorist outfits/extremists in Kashmir and indulge in senseless violence. Every terrorist in Jammu & Kashmir is a Muslim, though every Muslim is not a terrorist.

Political corruption on an epidemic/alarming scale is the direct result of dilution of values following the gradual break-up of the joint family system. Large numbers of cases are pending in the courts in all parts of India. The values

5. Vide T.N. Madan, *Family Kinship: A Study of The Pandits of Rural Kashmir*, Bombay: Asia Publishing House, 1965.

7 - Professor V.T. Patil, former Vice-Chancellor of Pondicherry University, presenting his paper

associated with the traditional joint family like simplicity, honesty of purpose and integrity are at a premium. The joint family system itself is under attack and on the wane.

The triangular nexus between bureaucracy, mafia and politicians is a deadly combination striking at the very root of value systems intrinsic to the traditional joint family system. The development of a new criminal culture, unique in itself, has added new dimension to corruption.

Another horrendous development in the last few years is criminalization of politics. It is reported that one-third of the members of the Indian parliament have criminal cases pending against them. It is even worse in the case of state legislatures in Uttar Pradesh and Bihar. Around 40 to 50 MLAs in each of these two states have criminal records. Certainly, it is a very depressing spectacle to observe that members of the parliament and the state legislatures who represent the sovereign will of the sovereign people of India indulge in criminal and other unlawful activities.

In recent years the sanctity of parliament and state legislatures has been considerably diluted and undermined by the unparliamentary and unruly behaviour of parliamentarians and state legislators. Legislative bodies represent the will of the people in a democracy and people's representatives are expected to engage in serious and meaningful discussion and debate. But, these sovereign bodies have been converted into noisy battlegrounds, many a time ending in unruly behaviour and physical assaults. The people's representatives are expected to maintain the dignity and decorum of these legislative bodies, but, on the other hand, the people are witness to unseemly spectacle/ scenes resembling a fish market. More often, these sovereign bodies representing the *sanctum sanctorum* of India's democracy are converted into battlegrounds by partisan members to achieve their dubious ends. These illustrations reflect adversely on the national character, which again is a result of the breakdown of the joint family system in India.

The most significant change in the joint family system under the impact of systemic and domestic forces is the dramatic transformation in the role and status of female members in the family. Prior to economic liberalization and accelerated growth women did not have a genuine opportunity to break age-old barriers of limited or lesser role in the society. For the first time, large numbers of women are progressively finding gainful employment in various professions. The stage is set for financial autonomy/ independence for women accompanied by general enhancement in their status and power within the family and the society. India has enacted progressive laws like property rights for women on par with men. Women are now poised to compete with men on a footing of equality for jobs in almost every profession. Women's empowerment is likely to receive greater fillip as and when parliament enacts legislation for 33 per cent reservation of seats for women in legislatures and parliament. As a result of these measures, women who earlier were dependent for financial security upon the joint family are now financially independent and assertive in family matters. The impact of this new development is weakening the patriarchal nature of the traditional Indian joint family.

Likewise, the privileged position of elders in the joint family is under attack because of the gradual withering away of joint family practices, norms and traditions. The elders now realize that the joint family no longer offers them financial security in their old age. The younger members move out of the joint family for jobs in distant places and the elders face difficulty in adjustment to nuclear families.

The Indian state realizing the changed context and consequent plight of the older generation has enacted laws fixing responsibilities on sons and daughters for providing maintenance to parents in their old age. The break-up of the traditional joint family system has destroyed the authority structure of the joint family. The nuclear family (by definition) — especially in urban areas — provides for a lesser or virtually no role for elders in the family.

The Constitution under Article 52 states that there "shall be a uniform civil code" in the country. For a number of reasons, mostly political in nature, successive governments have not implemented this constitutional provision in the last six decades. Some critics observe that no political party wants to displease the minorities, while others argue that the uniform civil code issue has become a casualty of party politics. Politicians neither think beyond their noses nor are they interested in out of box solutions. Their primary concern is with protection of their turfs, centring on party interests at the expense of the nation. For them, electoral politics has higher priority than larger societal interests. The failure to enact the uniform civil code for all religious communities is another reason for weakening of the joint family system. The moribund Hindu joint family system is not able to reinforce the need for a uniform civil code nor is it strong enough to preserve the existing delicate balance between the majority and minority communities. From a demographic perspective the percentage of Muslim (minority) population *vis-à-vis* the majority population has increased considerably in the last six decades.

Another important issue of recent origin is the fact that constitutional authorities like the office of the president and speaker have become subjects of controversy due to the play of power politics by political parties. Making these high constitutional offices controversial devalues/undermines the spirit and substance of Indian democracy. From this discussion it is evident that respect for authority is on the decline in a considerable measure, which corresponds to the simultaneous decline of the authority structure in the joint family system.

From time immemorial the argumentative tradition (in the West it corresponds to dialogue/discussion) is part of the s. This tradition served the Indian society very well in the past because conflicts were resolved amicably. In the joint family system the argumentative Indian tradition was adopted by the head of the family to discuss and resolve conflicts among members living under one roof. Unfortunately, the argumentative tradition imbibed from the past has degenerated into gossip mongering ("talking shop") and loose talk amounting to character assassination of individuals. We see this ugly spectacle in schools, colleges, universities, government offices and various other private institutions in the country. Hypocrisy also has become a common vice among the people, where transparent expression of ideas is uncommon because every other person likes to put his second thoughts first. Given this scenario, meaningful dialogue on serious issues of national concern to everybody becomes a very difficult proposition. Once again, misuse of argumentative tradition can be traced to the weakness of the joint family system, which has now become a moribund institution.

Caste system constituted an important part of the joint family system for long periods in Indian history. However, in recent years dramatic changes have reduced the salience of caste as a dominant or critical variable. In the north-eastern states, which are predominantly populated by tribes, and large tribal areas in Orissa, Chhattisgarh, Jharkhand, etc.

ethnic factors have supplanted the caste as a critical variable. The family structure and its operational dynamics are determined by ethnicity in these areas rather than caste and is a pointer to the changing nature or breakdown of traditional joint family system. Adequate and appropriate socialization process in the family system in these states is neither feasible nor possible. This major lacuna has resulted in emergence of the culture of violence and separatism in these areas.

The traditional joint family system will eventually break up into nuclear families and finally into post-nuclear families emerging with new characteristic features like single mother, same sex marriage, stepmother, stepfather, stepchildren (result of frequent divorce and remarriages), etc. The joint family system is withering away due to the relentless impact of globalization, modernization, exposure to Western ideology and consequential "demonstration effect" and rapid economic growth. The new and powerful forces are impacting on the traditional joint family. Accordingly, joint families are breaking into nuclear families in metropolitan and urban centres of India. The structure, substance and operational dynamics of the newly emerging nuclear families are different from the older set-up. Heterogeniety and gradation in hierarchy within the same caste has created a new sub-culture of sub-castes in the Hindu family system. This new development has further weakened the traditional joint family. Therefore, it is my considered view that it may be very difficult to redefine the Indian joint family in a manner that it continues to play a progressive role even in the face of powerful new realities. The joint family will decline and eventually wither away. It has lost its rationale and relevance after the almost universal emergence of the nuclear family model. Time, objective conditions and circumstances favour the nuclear family/post-nuclear family as the functional unit in society in the future.

The significance of enormous changes in the contemporary world and their impact on Indian family system must be examined carefully. Misperceptions must be avoided at all costs. In this great debate on Indian family system conceptual clarity or terminological exactitude is imperative for meaningful solutions to vexatious problems. In spite of enormous changes in the joint family system, the law still defines Indian family as "Hindu undivided family." Any law worth its name must reflect social reality. Unfortunately, the existing law suffers from inadequacies which further aggravates the difficulties of the Indian family system.

The Constitution clearly enjoins the Indian state to have uniform civil code. Here again nothing seems to have been done to put the constitutional requirement into a law.

Yet another problem relates to the terms "joint family" and "household." A perusal of existing writings on Indian family points to the fact that proper distinction is not made between a joint family and a household. Quite often, the two terms are used interchangeably. Lack of conceptual clarity becomes a bottleneck, preventing objective discussion and dialogue on an ancient social institution which provided strength and meaning to Indian civilization. Whatever the nature of changes in the structure and substance of the new family system, values like compassion, tolerance, flexibility, and respect for authority, honesty and ethics must constitute the intrinsic baggage of any new dispensation.

Our discussion on the changing contours of the Indian joint family system and its impact mostly supports the four hypotheses specified in the beginning of the essay. In terms of our analytical discussion the first hypothesis is affirmed in the sense that in a society in the process of transition from tradition to modernity, values, beliefs and practices of the joint family system undergo major changes. The second hypothesis that momentous systemic changes like globalization, modernization and the Information Technology revolution are bound to have a powerful impact on the structure and substance of the joint family system is also supported by our critical discussion. The third hypothesis stating that the joint family system is heading towards a break-up into a nuclear or post-nuclear family due to rapid economic growth is proved by the fact that nuclear families are a prominent feature in urban areas of India (metropolitan cities and towns). The last hypothesis which states that the joint family system, as it gets transformed, eventually triggers social crises and endemic violence devaluing some of the established institutions of the society has also been affirmed by our discussion.

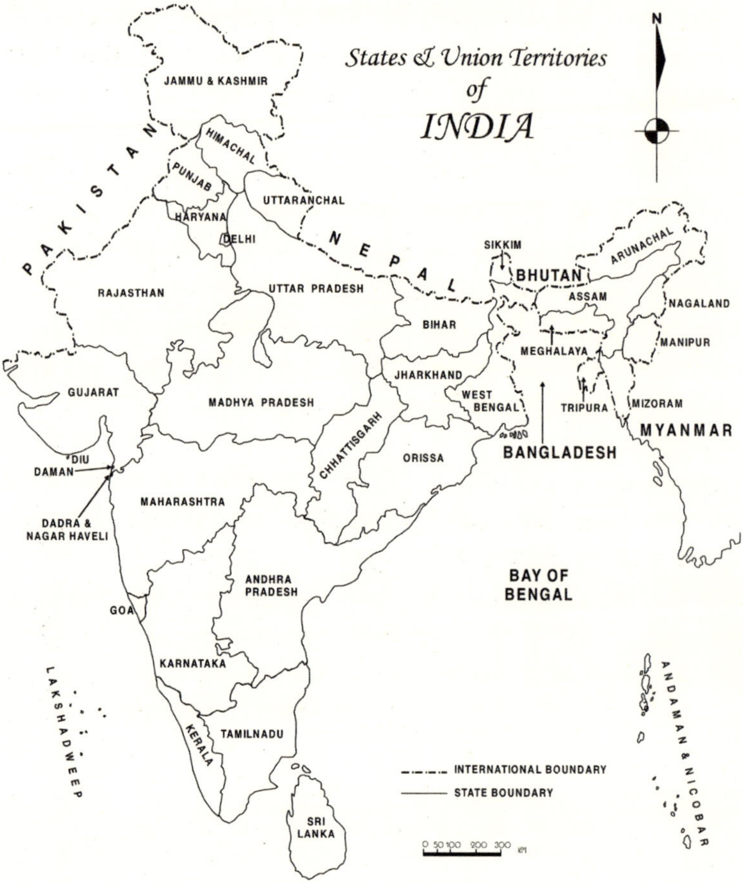
States & Union Territories
of
INDIA
N
JAMMU & KASHMIR
PAKISTAN
HIMACHAL
PUNJAB
UTTARANCHAL
HARYANA
DELHI
NEPAL
SIKKIM
BHUTAN
ARUNACHAL
RAJASTHAN
UTTAR PRADESH
ASSAM
NAGALAND
BIHAR
MEGHALAYA
MANIPUR
GUJARAT
JHARKHAND
MADHYA PRADESH
WEST BENGAL
TRIPURA
MIZORAM
CHHATTISGARH
MYANMAR
DIU
DAMAN
ORISSA
BANGLADESH
MAHARASHTRA
DADRA & NAGAR HAVELI
ANDHRA PRADESH
BAY OF BENGAL
GOA
KARNATAKA
LAKSHADWEEP
ANDAMAN & NICOBAR
KERALA
TAMILNADU
INTERNATIONAL BOUNDARY
STATE BOUNDARY
SRI LANKA
0 50 100 200 300 KM

Traditional Joint Family

Large Traditional Joint Family

Nuclear Family

Hindu Marriage

Sikh Marriage

Muslim Marriage

Christian Marriage

Hindu Temple

Christian Church

Sikh Gurdwara

Muslim Mosque

5

Gārhasthya (Household), the Supreme Moral Ideal

A Path to Śreyas (Ought)

D.R. Satapathy
Gautama Satapathy

The paper discusses *gārhasthya* as the central construct of the Indian family system that unites the two extreme but irreducibly accommodative stages of *brahmacarya* and *vānaprastha*. By the way the paper provides a critique of the key concepts of Indian ethical nuances such as *śreyas, preyas, svadharma, tapaḥ, ācāra, śraddhā, puruṣārtha, lokasaṁgraha, sthitaprajña*, etc. their role and the position in the Indian *āśrama* of *gārhasthya* extending its domain by inevitability to civilization, culture, history, moral, social and spiritual life including society and governance.

FAMILY in India is a moral institution where a householder with his spouse assumes a holy marital responsibility by practising the omnipotent ideals of *śraddhā, svadharma, ṛta* and *puruṣārtha* together as *dampati*. The paper emphasizes the attainment of *śreyas* (the good) through discrimination the householder is commanded to realise ultimate emancipation or *mokṣa* with accompanying virtues *satya, jñāna, ahiṁsā, tapaḥ, ārjava, ācāra* and the final consummation in *sthitaprajña*, the unique spiritual existence towards the goal of world family (*vasudhaivakuṭumbakam*).

The essay analyses critically the Indian family concept which arises during epic periods and the Purāṇas. The discussion also has taken into consideration the aspects of the literary and aesthetic parallels of the ethical and the social good that *gārhasthya* essentially upholds. The essay concludes with alternative outlooks of the ancient and the modern-colonial India as it projects them through the family system. It hopes that modern culture which has been victim of crises of consciousness can find answers in the Indian heritage which focuses on family unification fused with social unification, towards global unification that machine age has neglected.

I

> *śreyaśca preyaśca manuṣyametastau samparītya vivinakti dhīraḥ*
>
> Both the good and pleasant approach a man. The wise ponders over them, discriminates. — *Kaṭha Up.*, 1.2.2

The paper critically evaluates the divide between "pleasurable" (*preyas*) and "preferable" (*śreyas*)[1] from the Indian familial perspective. The very discussion stems from a misunderstanding between a father and a son which took place in the dialogue of *Kaṭhopaniṣad.* Vājaśravas, the protagonist of external ceremonialism who insisted on *preyas* and Nachiketas, the son, who persists on spiritual wisdom, *śreyas,* as the essay contests these two key factors here. In the conflict presented between these two ideologies *Kaṭha* disclosing the path-breaking truth that is in *śreyas,* the good, lies the essence of humanity and spiritual wisdom.

---

1. Please see more about the parallel of "pleasurable" and "preferable" equated with "is" and "ought" in Alasdair MacIntyre, *After Virtue*, London: Gerald Duckworth.

The paper is based on this high cultural paradigm of Indian heritage. Nachiketas's visit to Yama[2] in order to know the *śreyas* figures in the epoch-making dialogue about family life. This carries significance for family life which distinguishes and empowers one to grow with truth as failing to "distinguish" one falls to destruction,

iha ced avedīd atha satyamasti
na ced ihāvedīn mahatī vinaṣṭiḥ | — *Kena*, II.5

This very ideal relates to man's highest accomplishment of *sthitaprajña*, a worldly ideal that the *Gītā* glorifies. *Gārhasthya* opens a forum for making a decision between eternal and ephemeral[3] which is the *raison d'être* of Indian cultural heritage.

This ideal practice appeared in practical and applied form in society as in everyday habit and behaviour with the literature that emerged with Smṛtis which constitute the strong foundation of the texts from Manu to Parāśara, Yājñavalkya to Āpastamba, Gobhila and Hiraṇyakeśin. The essential notions of these Smṛtis relate to ideals of *ācāra, tapaḥ, puruṣārtha*, and the *trivarga*. These familial ideals have significance in Indic civilization which developed with passages of time in their modern approach during colonial period by social reformers like Rammohun Roy, Sri Ramakrishna, Dayananda Saraswati and Annie Besant.[4] There are scientific and socio-ethical dimensions of this doctrine which essentially surface in the abolition of *satī*, child-marriage, caste and colour prejudice and conflict among religions. The ideals of *varṇāśrama dharma* also underwent alterations in the changing face of time

2. The God of Death.
3. *Nitya* and *Anitya*.
4. All these relate to the movement like Brahmo Samāj, Ramakrishna Mission, Ārya Samāj to Sādhāraṇa Samāj and the Theosophical Society.

with the intention of the welfare of the people (*lokasaṁgraha*), thus leading to a renaissance of humanism of which Indic culture and civilization is the forerunner.

II

Gārhasthya, the Nucleus of Indian Family System

Gārhasthya is not just *āśrama dharma* as a truism but a pattern of faith and a path of realization of *śreyas*. It dismisses the idea of the individual as a free windowless agent.[5] Rather it portrays selfless sacrifice, having love and concern for the neighbour which makes a wholesome human person. Here *lokasaṁgraha* (social concern) and *dharma* play as the *raison d'être* and a power that binds a *gārhasthya* ideal into a family system. The meagre microcosmic man here assumes a higher personalistic profile along with a role in citizenship. Thus from this citizenship he grows to an enlightened citizen, participating in global governance and international commune. In such a new assignment he forgets himself as a pure individual, narrow and dwarfish.

GṚHASTHA AND GṚHIṆĪ: THE DEFINITION OF THE CONCEPT

Gṛhastha can be said to be a genetically determined concept. It centres in the *gṛha* or home. The *gṛha* is associated with *gṛhiṇī* (the housewife) and vice versa. *Gṛhiṇī* plays a significant role in *gṛhastha dharma*, "wife is verily a home, of one heart and perfect concord," declare the Vedas (*ṚV*, 1.183.1-2, *Atharvaveda*, 3.30). The mother at home is verily the mother of civilizations, announce all Dharmaśāstras, whether Manu, Parāśara, Yājñavalkya or Āpastamba. She is *jāyā*,[6] a theory of evolution of biological and psychophysical non-duality, as described here.

5. Monad.

6. The husband becoming embryo is borne by her.

patirbhāryām sampraviśya garbhobhūtaeha jayate
jāyayātaddhi jāyatvam yadasyām jāyate punaḥ । — *Manu*, IX.8

PATH TO ŚREYAS

Gārhasthya is accepted as the institution to practise the higher goals of life. It is the cradle of social human understanding, love and mutual goodness. In accomplishing these virtues together in a harmonious companionship, husband and wife are called *dampati* (*jāyācapatiśca*). *Dharma* (religious duty) *ṛta*[7] (universal order) fulfilling *āśrama*s and the *puruṣārtha*s becomes their forte. A lifelong fidelity and unity is breathed between them providing the greatest clue towards feminist understanding. This relation *sui generis*, the righteous union between husband and wife has a momentous result, soon catapults to an explosive pattern with the next richer rank in *vānaprastha*. It is a stage of courage and fearlessness which carries the signature of eternal partnership to join the sweet delight at home and austere and the demanding life in the forest dwelling.

MORAL LADDER: BRAHMACARYA, KEY TO GĀRHASTHYA

Indian heritage discovers a constant ascent in moral ladder. It is not a biological evolution but a psychosocial evolution as post-Darwinian like Julian Huxley discovers it. Family here thus emerges as a spiritual concept in India from the four-dimensional hierarchy of living. *Brahmacarya* evolves into *gārhasthya* as inevitable stage. The life of rigorous academic discipline of *brahmacarya* forms the seed and the impetus to grow into plant of *gṛhasthya* with flowers, foliage and fruit of *karma* along with its results. In *brahmacarya* the pupils live in the residential colony with the teacher, sharing not only intellectual food but also physical food. Such order of sacred pursuit of knowledge builds a strong fortress to encounter the life to come in the *gṛhastha dharma*. The family life which is

7. The moral order.

religiously associated and follows the studenthood makes household a righteous stage. In studenthood the entire attention is given to build complete personality with physical, mental, moral and spiritual growth. Along with the texts also the curriculum includes the ethical and moral studies of *satyam, tapaḥ, damaḥ,* tranquillity (*samaḥ*), *āgneya* (the sacrificial fire), sacrifice (*agnihotra*), *ātithya* (respect for guests), humanity (*mānuṣam*) and significantly offspring *prajāḥ*), begetting (*prajanaḥ*) and propagation (*prajātiḥ*). *Taittirīya Upaniṣad* enunciates these series of evolving technique:

ṛtamca svādhyāya pravacaneca
satyamca tapaśca pravacaneca
prajāca svādhyāya pravacaneca
prajanaḥ svādhyāya pravacaneca
prajātiḥ svādhyāya pravacaneca

The last three stages are direct rationale to *gārhasthya* to generate and beget offspring and propagate. Thus *gārhasthya* is not only a biological compulsion but also a socio-ethical compulsion. *Gārhasthya* opens the doors to an exalted career that man enters into and from which platform with a complete background of ethical, moral and aesthetic as he can bravely utter with the exalted voice of Triśaṅku.

ahaṁ vṛkṣasya rerivā

I am the mover of the (world) tree,

kīrtiḥ pṛṣṭhaṁ gireriva

My fame is like mountain peak. — *Taittirīya,* 1.10.1

From these follow many ethical exhortations.[8]

---

8. Which is imparted to the departing students which form as guidelines to the life in the next *āśrama — satyam vada, dharmam cara, svādhāya mā pramadaḥ,* and the last, the link to *gṛhasthāśrama — prajātantum mā myavatchetsi.*

Humanly perfect, divinely audacious, worshipping mother as god, worshipping father as god, worshipping teacher as god, worshipping guest as God, *mātṛdevo bhava, pitṛdevo bhava, atithidevo bhava* and other lessons of conduct —

yan yanavadyāni karmāṇi | *tāni sevitavyāni* | *no itarāṇi* |
yān yasmākaṁ sucaritāni, tāni tvayā upāsyāni, no itarāṇi |
— *Taitt*, 1.11.2

The next lessons constitute of alms-giving, i.e. what is to be given is to be given with faith, should not be given without faith like Jesus exhorting, "let not your left hand know what your right hand doeth." Also we can cite here the classical example of Karṇa of the *Mahābhārata*, the great giver, to give in plenty and to give all [who had the capacity to give even to gods (Indra)] — *śraddhyā deyam, aśraddhyā deyam śriyā deyam, sambhidā deyam*, the genesis of behaviourist ethics. *Gārhasthya* thus impeccably seems to constitute a noble human model that will beget the global model of *vasudhaivakuṭumbakam*.

WOMAN AT HOME

As stated earlier wife is verily the home, as the *Mahābhārata* corroborates —

na gṛham gṛhamityāhu, gṛhiṇī gṛhamucyate |
gṛham tu gṛhiṇī hīnam āraṇya sadṛśam matam ||

These ideas have powerful symbolic expressions in Lord Śiva's icon as Ardhanārīśvara, man sharing the woman manifestation, imbibing woman's characteristic features. Pārvatī's deep attachments to the sons, one of which has great intellectual power, another having unbeatable prowess and Śiva as the father is the epitome of householder as *sthitaprajña*, *yogī* symbolizing the Indian head of family.

Śruti and Smṛti, Purāṇas and epics and all literatures from the Vedas to Kālidāsa, Bhavabhūti to Śrīharṣa voice in authoritative tone the significance and value of *gārhasthya.* This can be said to be the Indian contribution to the world culture as the omnipotent man-making stage. Even heretical literature of Buddhism, Jainism and materialistic Cārvāka are equally vocal about it.

III

Family, a Unit of Social System

Family as a unit of social system is the greatest gift of India to the world civilization. It has got unique function in ancient India which is inconceivable in the contemporary period. Family includes parents, children and their descendants. There exist joint families including father-mother, even stepmother and stepchildren and not excluding adapted children and domestic servants, serfs and sometimes includes students.

MANU ON FAMILY

Manu in his *Mānava-Dharma-Śāstra* talks of family in the following lines:

> Having bathed with the permission of his teacher and performed according to the rules of *samāvartana* (the rites of returning home) a twice born man shall marry a wife of equal caste who is endowed with auspicious bodily marks. Let him wed a female free from bodily defects, who has an agreeable name, the graceful gait of swan (*haṁsa*) or of an elephant (*vāraṇa*), a moderate quantity of hair on body and head, and small teeth and soft limbs.

> *abyaṅgāṅgī saumyanāmnī haṁsavāraṇagāminīm* |
> *tanulomakeśadasanam mṛdaṅgī mṛdvahet priyam* || — 3.10

A damsel who is neither a *sapiṇḍa* on the mothers' side, nor belongs to the same family on the father's side is recommended for wedlock and conjugal union. This marital principle has important biological significance which provides a topic for important research justifying contemporary conjugal, medical, and scientific theories.

Indian family constitution has two more beautiful organizations called *śrāddha* and joint family system which epitomize love, brotherhood, solidarity, and other variegated characters in superb concourse. In *śrāddha*, a rite of commemorating the ancestors, balls of rice called *piṇḍa*s are offered. The sons, grandsons and the great-grandsons of the deceased join together to make this offering to the three generations of the dead which is a unique phenomenon.

MARRIAGE WHICH FORMS THE PIVOT OF GĀRHASTHYA

Manu enumerates eight kinds of marriage, with five kinds of sacrifices and three ends of life. To start from the end, the three kinds of values for the householders assigned are *dharma, artha* and *kāma*; religious, economic and aesthetic good. The eight kinds of marriages are *brāhma* marriage, marriage to same class; *daiva* marriage, householder offering his daughter to the priest as a fee; *ārṣa* marriage, with cow and bulls as dowry; *prājāpatya* marriage as father giving his daughter without dowry; *gandharva* marriage is love marriage based on mutual consent; *asura* marriage is marriage by purchase; *rākṣasa*, marriage by capture; and last is *piśāca*, by seduction — last is the worst of all. The *pañca-mahāyajñas* are *brahma-yajña* by reciting Vedas, *deva-yajña* by pouring ghee on sacrificial fire, *pitṛ-yajña* is worshipping of ancestors with libation by water, *bhūta-yajña* is scattering food for animals and birds and lastly, *puruṣa-yajña* as showing hospitality to people. They are practised just to ward off the evils or to purify the inner self. These ideas have great significance for not only socio-scientific research but for opening the gateway to new social understanding.

The eight kinds of marriage have deep sociological

implications. Of the eight the first four are lawful for the brāhmaṇa, and the last four for kṣatriya, vaiśya, and the śūdra. The *piśāca* marriage has all along been denounced as sinful. Children born out of these marriages present gradations of greater or lesser qualities. In the blameless marriages are born blameless children, in blameable, the blameable offsprings which the later and the modern social scientists may attribute to be the cause of social imbalance, terrorism, war, conflict, fear, violence and other evils.

The Smr̥tis lay more importance on the woman's character who is the mother at home and mother of civilization. The *Bhagavad-Gītā* takes the cue as to how a bad home gives rise to illegitimate children associated to social evils (*strīsu duṣṭasu barṣneya jayate varṇa saṅkaraḥ*). Thus the social balance hinges on the quality of women — for the reason therefore Manu's oft-quoted line, *yatra nāryastu pūjyante ramante tatra devatāḥ*. (3.56). Where women are honoured there gods dwell and where they are not honoured no sacred rite yields rewards. Women must be honoured and adored by their fathers, brothers, husbands and brothers-in-law. Where female relations live in grief, the family soon wholly perishes. Hence he concludes, men who seek their own welfare should always honour women on holidays and festivals with gift of ornaments, clothes, and dainty food.

AESTHETIC FIELD

Gārhasthya has not only been the field where socio-political, ethical, cultural life should nurture and grow but also provide the fountain of human aesthetic accomplishments. Vātsyāyana, the great author of *Kāmasūtra* points to four kinds of women on the basis of their physical, psychic and aesthetic aptitude — *padminī, śaṅkhinī, hastinī* and *citriṇī*. Since the conception of home here is exemplary of refined and superior living along with practice of religious purity as well as aesthetic delight then Vātsyāyana's text can be considered to be the guide book for every householder.

Yājñavalkya beholds householder's life to be the greatest among all the stages of life, because in this life one can perform the duties enjoined by the Vedas. It is the stage or *āśrama* which is the support of all other *āśrama*s, though each *āśrama* has its own prescribed duties including ten *dharma*s — forbearance (*dhṛti*), forgiveness (*kṣamā*), mental control (*dama*), non-stealing (*asteya*), purity (*śauca*), sense control (*indriya nigraha*), wisdom (*dhī*), learning (*vidyā*), truthfulness (*satya*), and *akrodha* (absense of anger). Yājñavalkya continues that if a householder practises carefully these ten *dharma*s and properly listens to the Upaniṣads and practises self-abnegation, he attains final liberation. Such person by abnegating all fruits of *karma* is released from the defects of *karma*. Having done so he continually reads the Vedas, remains well cared for by his son and is detached from all things.[9]

Home life guarantees not only pure love but also protection and health, sanctity of life that helps the growth of good society. Great literature and books have been composed only against the background of a stable home.

GĀRHASTHYA IN INDIAN LITERATURE

Kālidāsa[10] can be portrayed as a perfectionist and as a symbol of poetic beauty and literary grandeur. The depiction of woman which combines external quality and inner sweetness as portrayed in Kālidāsa's Śakuntalā, Pārvatī and Vālmīki's Sītā can be studied parallel to Shakespeare's Miranda and Cleopatra, Dante's Beatrice and Homer's Helen. Indian poets

9. *Yājñavalkya-Smṛti* 94.96.

10. Kālidāsa can be best understood as Michelangelo of the East.

insist, where there is beauty there is the good (*śreyas*), (*surūpā suguṇā bhavanti*). Indian home asserts the simultaneous presence of aesthetics and ethics in unison as the *sine qua non* to *gārhasthya*.

IV

The Crises

Abhijñānaśākuntalam portrays the negligence of duty and discipline along with the moral aspect that a woman loving her husband must not disregard the ethics of entertaining guests (*puruṣa yajña*) due to which she suffered the curse from Durvāsā and again in order to atone for her sin she had to undergo long years of penance and exile till she comes back to join her husband Duṣyanta to a sacred home life. It goes without saying that "home" brought this great country to the birth of *Bhāratavarṣa* after the name of her son Bharata. In the next masterwork *Meghadūtam* of Kālidāsa, the case of Yakṣa's exile is a portrayal of another variety of family crisis, the separation. Pārvatī's penance for a home life with immortal husband Śiva is the subject matter of *Kumārasambhavam* which contains a crisis of different origin. All the literatures of India relate someway or the other to *gārhasthya* life. The unity and solidarity between man and wife even in time of joy or in time of suffering, curse or exile has been beautifully portrayed in *Naiṣadhīyacaritam* by Śrīharṣa. Here Nala and Damayantī suffer the exile being punished by Saturn God and it is amazing to know how heroically with moral fortitude they have overcome and come back to renew their home — a signpost of India's greatness of *gārhasthya* as supreme *dharma*.

I can make a reference to the great geniuses as the gift of *gṛhasthya* discipline, like Yājñavalkya (the wisest among men), Janaka (the philosopher king), Āruṇi and Triśaṅku (the great spiritual adventurers), Śāṇḍilya and Dadhīci (philosophers *par excellence*), Gautama (the greatest Naiyāyika) and many more are great householders.

CRISES IN INDIAN FAMILY CULTURE, THE RĀMĀYAṆA

Modern society is passing through great turmoil. It is the home which essentially disciplines and replenishes the loss of the balance. In India the two epics have shown how value crisis at home has led it to perils of innumerable proportions. This relates to the darkest crisis ever in the *Rāmāyaṇa*, the emotional crisis of Daśaratha and crises of confidence in Rāma. Being lost to the temptation for women Daśaratha lost his life and brought discredit to his kingdom. In the process Rāma was banished without fault and without strong reason and afterwards in Uttara-Kāṇḍa, Sītā, the purity incarnate, was banished being an object of suspicion, and what followed, the war between father and the son which pose a great ethical enigma.

THE MAHĀBHĀRATA, ETHICS AT CROSSROAD

The same parallels of peril could be drawn from the *Mahābhārata*. The whole of the *Mahābhārata* is painted on the background of indescribable family crises in every level from beginning till the end. The epic began with an original sin, as it were as Śāntanu, the king forced an uncalled-for marriage of a fisher-maid and prior to that he had developed a strained relation with Gaṅgā, the mother of Bhīṣma. This resulted in snowballing of crises from families to families. Dhṛtarāṣṭra accepted his blindness physically and also by conscience which led to their routing in the battle and the catastrophe. On the other side the divine offsprings Pāṇḍavas too had their errors of the unconscious with virgin mother Kuntī who can be said to be responsible for inverse polygamy with Draupadī which was an uncalled-for crisis to Indian cultural life, which of course subverted the structure of home. The seed lies in the family which even God could not save and has to take a part in order to hasten the end of the wrong that accumulated from time to time.

The Vedic religion contains a high watermark of family purity, bliss and beatitude as in contrast we have also antitheses in the epics and Purāṇas. Closer for ethical evaluation is *Dakṣa-Yajña,* Pārvatī's death, Śiva wreaking havoc.

Conclusion

While discussing the family system in India we must weigh both sides of pleasurable and preferable as the key nuances as discussed earlier. However, the contemporary crises could be studied against the extraordinary invasion of Western culture into Indian family system. The contemporary generation and the social change as also change in the family structure and the changes in family relations between parents and children which figure as a matter of great concern deserve re-evaluation.[11]

Gārhasthya is not the monopoly of a place or a nation, rather it is something which could be claimed by mankind. From the mundane perspective, if we can analyse, who does not aspire for a life of pleasure, family-feeling and sweetness of social relations? From this point of view India too leads the world ethos. However, every culture has its own crises, and India has withstood the crises due to constant confrontation against its own cultural bottlenecks as well as external invasions and has come up with flying colours due to its ancestry and strong roots entrenched in the Vedas, the Vedāṅgas, Smṛtis, the Epics along with essence of literature. The nutriment of cultural heritage makes it the best of all the world cultures and family

---

11. Charles Taylor, *Malaises of Modernity*, the emergence of atomistic family, me generations, permissive society and loosing the great chain of being so on and so forth describes the whole crises.

systems. Family systems which are in disarray around the globe are still intact in India. Whatever may be the nature and the character of invasion of the Western culture, it has stayed unperturbed till now irrespective of locations whether in Africa or Antarctica because it exists inside and outside us in many manifestations irrespective of our daily life, living, ritual or family relationships.

References

Basham, A.L., *The Wonder That Was India*, Rupa, 1987.

Duessen, Paul, *Philosophy of the Upanishads*, N.Y.: Dover, 1906.

Ghose, B.K., *Hindu Ideal of Life*, Calcutta: Satischandra Seal, 1947.

Kane, P.V., *History of Dharmashastra*, Pune: Bhandarkar Oriental Research Institute, 1930-1962.

Macdonnel, A.A., *History of Sanskrit Literature*, London: D. Appleton & Co., 1st edn., 1900.

Max Müller, F.H., The Sacred Books of the East, New Delhi: Motilal Banarsidass, 1997, vols. 25, 29, 30, 32, 40, 42 and 46.

Radhakrishnan, S., *Eastern Religions and Western Thought*, New York: Oxford University Press, 1959.

———, *The Principal Upanishads*, New Delhi: Oxford University Press, 1992.

Ranade, R.D., *A Constructive Survey of Upanishadic Philosophy*, Bombay: Bharatiya Vidya Bhawan Press, 1986.

Sengupta, N., *Evolution of Hindu Marriage*, Bombay: Popular Prakashan, 1965.

Valavalkar, P.H., *Hindu Social Institutions*, Calcutta: Longmans & Green, 1939.

Vātsyayāna, *The Kāmasūtra*, Wendy Doniger and Sudhir Kakav, Oxford: Oxford University Press, 2002.

Walavalakar, P.H., "Hindu Social Institutions," in K.M. Kapadia Hindu Kinship an important Chapter in Hindu Social History, Bombay : Popular Book Depot, 1947.

Williams, Monier-William, *Indian Wisdom*, New Delhi: Rupa & Co.

Winternitz, M., tr. S. Ketkar, *History of Indian Literature*, Delhi: Motilal Banarsidass, 1981.

8 - V.D. Misra, Head of Sociology Department,
Lucknow University, presenting his paper

6

Indian Family System
A Sociological Encounter

V.D. Misra

MAN is a cultural animal[1] and had started community life even before the evolution of language.[2] Though the primitive man did not differ much from other animals, his inquisitive nature and constant questioning enabled him to unravel the secrets of natural forces and to control them. Gradually the zeal for knowledge and ever-increasing inquisitiveness gathered momentum and, finally, man assumed supremacy over nature. Agriculture was developed by the human beings in the next stage of their cultural evolution, when they had properly settled down, leaving behind the mobile days of nomadic life,[3] in a more stable family way.

Thus family has always been the foremost biological and social necessity. It is the cultural unit of society which can be called sub-system[4] or miniature organism of society. It gives the societal moorings to the individual. We all know man is a

1. R.M. McIvor and C.H. Page, *Society*, London: Macmillan, 1976, p. 41.
2. H.S. Lucas, *A Short History of Civilization*, New York: McGraw Hill Book Co. Incorporation, 1943, pp. 7-8.
3. G.D. Mitchell, *Sociology*, Delhi: Oxford University Press, 1970, p. 55.
4. Edward Westermarck, *History of Human Marriage*, vol. I, London: Macmillan, 1921, Chap. I, p. 26.

group entity and since time immemorial, he cherishes the boons of togetherness and group support, but it was a biological compulsion as well. Being physically weak man can't survive in loneliness.[5] Later it developed into community feelings and finally as family organization. This organization had seen many facets of emerging new value patterns. In the beginning it might not have affected much but in days following it became the real genesis of family life with marriage as the fundamental social structure of family system. Man is undivided biological individual at the time of birth, it is family which develops him into a socially responsible individual. After birth a person comes into the contact with other persons and by the means of communication mimic, he internalizes the attitudes and thoughts of other persons. By the process of socialization a person learns the ideals of society transforming him into a social individual. Family plays most important roles in all these processes and shaping personality of newborn child according to the family value system. No doubt this impact gradually minimized after attaining the maturity but in the primary stage it plays very important role in bringing up and rearing of the child. It is rightly said that family is the first school of every individual.

The social structure of primitive and advanced patriarchal societies was entirely made up of family units. In India also the Vedic families were the basic units of society in which the eldest of the family (*kula*) was the family chief and named as *kulapati*.[6] The Vedic community consisted of an aggregation of so many *kula*s. Aristotle[7] also supported the same argument and said community was the group of families.

5. W.G. Sumner, *Folkways*, New York: Ginn, 1906, pp. 348-49.
6. *Ṛgveda*, X.179.2.
7. Aristotle, Brainy Quote.com, explore Inc. 2010.

Family is the most important institution which provides continuity to the existence of society.[8] Every social order has certain values and to continue these values society needs unbreakable continuity. The family system provides assurance and gives permanent solution to this basic need in the form of progeny. In the Indian context it is the fundamental responsibility of every household to protect the progeny. Family not only provides space for it but also organizes and facilitates the conditions required for childbirth. It also gives a particular status to the newborn child for future role. So it is also a status-giving agency. Every individual gets a status in the society to fulfil certain social rights and duties. And the existence of society depends upon adherence of these social duties and rights. Society is thus a functional whole which always requires the fulfilment of social responsibilities from its members. Every component has to fill the vacant places also which come through the loss of its members, as death is certain and a continuous process. So the progeny should also be organized in the same way by the society and it was the foremost contribution of family towards society.[9]

Family is such an organization which can be called universal. At every stage of development, right from primitive days, we find some or other form of family. When marriage had not originated, people used to live in a group formation and behave like members of a big family. Later on with the advent of marriage, group organization divided in the manifold system, people were bound in so many systems like monogamy, polygamy or polyandry which all give support

---

8. T. Parsons, and Rober F. Bales, *Family Socialization and Interaction Process*, Glencose: The Free Press, 1985, p. 7.
9. Edward Westermarck, *History of Human Marriage*, vol. I, London: Macmillan, 1921, Chap. I, p. 19.

and opportunity to the children to grow and brighten the future of the organization.

Family has also given the shape for fulfilment of basic life requirement and occupation pattern which ultimately organized the tenets of culture. It is like the situation of basis and superstructure. Being a group species, men were bound to live in groups as it was biological defensive mechanism, but every group has certain understanding or requirements which are supposed to be complied by its members as essentials of groups. This primitive group understanding paved the way for social moorings and later on as value system, which ultimately helped in the formation of cultural pattern. Nature expands on the basis of differentiation and in accordance with every country has somehow developed a system of altogether different culture. Family system plays a crucial role in the making of cultural moorings according to the social needs and finally becomes cradle of cultural pattern. We find family in every culture but on different footings, playing the maximum role in the formation of personality as a whole.

The diversity of family system can be seen in the form of mating relationships. Marriage may be permanent or temporary, it may manifest in group marriage, monogamy or polygamy, is a universal phenomenon.[10] Reckoning of descent is provided by the family system. Selection of spouse and its types are also provided by the marriage. The rules regarding the marriage are result of this functional necessity. Because of culture differentiation, family took many forms with a variety of regulation and multiple types of marriage. It also created differences in aims and objectives among various communities and unstablility to the structure.

---

10. H. Vedalankar, *Hindū Parivāra Mīmāṁsā*, Mussoorie: Saraswati Sadan, 1963, p. 1.

The universal definition of family is very difficult because of its perpetually changing form and significance. It may relish different shapes and positions in the same society. We may think of a married couple only or with children, married males and females with their children or widow woman with children or alone and a widower in the same situation.[11] All these are the forms of individual families. Thus we can say, family is more or less a durable association of husband and wife, with or without children, or of a man or woman alone, or with children.

Marriage is usually referred as a social institution,[12] but it does not denote a perfect social institution, and, therefore, not a fully correct assertion. Marriage has no structure. "The family is the institution, and it was antecedent to marriage." The marriage has always been an elastic and variable usage. In fact, the use of language reflects the vagueness of marriage, for we use the word "marriage" for wedding, nuptials or matrimony (wedlock). Only the last can be termed an institution.[13]

Marriage had played very important role in the formation of stable family system which can be explained as more or less an organization where people get opportunity of sex satisfaction and progeny, and have the proper time to grow their children. As such family is a group defined by sex relationship sufficiently precise and enduring to provide for the procreation and upbringing of children. The biological

---

11. Denial Larner, *The Passing of Traditional Society*, London: Free Press, 1958, p. 23.
12. Ogburn and Nimkaff, *A Hand Book of Sociology*, New Delhi: Eurasia Publishing House (Pvt.) Ltd., p. 438.
13. Ibid, p. 439.

dependence of children is the cause of enduring necessity of marriage.

The terms of families can be classified into two major categories where husband and wife with children live together in the permanent form, and is known as the family of procreation, nuclear family, natured family, individual family or modern family, while others were known as extended families including joint family with or without polygamy and polyandry.[14]

Indian family system is more complex because of its *varṇa* (caste) system and religious involvement. The joint family is the basic tenet of Indian family organization. It was cherished even in Vedic days as well as in modern times. In the Vedic period the newly married couples were supposed to live in the husband's father's house.

उहैव स्तं मा वियोष्ठं विश्वमायुर्व्यश्नुतम्।
क्रीडन्ती पुत्रैर्नप्तृभिमोदमानी स्वे गृहै।।[15]

uhaiva staṁ mā viyoṣṭhaṁ viśvamāyurvyaśnutam ।
krīḍantī putrairnaptṛbhimodamānī sve gṛhai ।।

The above verse desires from newly married couple:

> don't go elsewhere, live here up to whole life playing with your children and grandchildren joyfully.

This verse is so important that it has been made the part of marriage ceremony and pronounced at the time of actual ceremony other verses also support the same feelings.

श्वसुरे सम्राज्ञीभव श्वश्रवा सम्राज्ञीभव।
नन्दान्दरि सम्राज्ञीभव सम्राज्ञी अधिदेवृषु।।[16]

---

14. MacIvor and Page, *Society*, London: Macmillan, 1976.
15. *Ṛgveda* (X.85.42), Bareilly: Sanskriti Sansthan, 1967.
16. Ibid, X.85.46.

śvasure samrājñībhava śvaśravā samrājñībhava |
nandāndari samrājñībhava samrājñī adhidevṛṣu | |

You should be the queen above mother, father, sister and brother of your husband.

All these verses show that joint family was very much liked and prevalent in Vedic period.

Generally the joint family requires common living, common kicthen, common purse, common belief, and a blood relationship among its members. A joint family is a group of people who generally live under one roof, who eat food cooked at one hearth, who hold property in common and who participate in common worship and are related to each other as some particular type of kindred.[17] We can give more elaborated and advanced definition: "we call that household a joint family which is related to one another by property, income and the mutual right and obligations."[18] The sharing of mutual rights and obligation is the basis of modern joint families who are not necessarily under the same roof because of modern requirements of lifestyle, studies and occupation. In spite of living at different places, cities and even in other countries people of joint families share mutual sentiments and try to participate and help when required.

Indian joint families have taken a new shape in its extensive form. It has joint feelings of happiness and sorrow. They up to some extent maintain the position of common fund. Elder persons behave like trustees of the property and try to help each family member. It is some sort of family socialism where

17. David G. Mandelbaum, *The Family in India*, Ruth Nanda Anshen, New York: Harper and Brother, p. 167.

18. I. Karve, *Kinship Organization in India*, Bombay: Asia Publishing House, 1965, p. 10.

each person contributes to his ability and finds according to his needs.[19]

In Indian family system the nucleus is made by the relationship between husband and wife. It may have children and parents or other dependents of family or earning dependents also. But all have some relationship and mutual feelings of dependency.[20] The ideal family chief (*mukhiyā*) maintains organismic unity in family and behaves like the mouth of family, which takes food but distributes it according to the needs of different organs. Though polygamy was also not discarded but the ideal was monogamy. Marriage is not ceremonized as an opportunity of pleasure but as a start of bearing the higher responsibilities of family life. The word *vivāha* stands for the bearing (*vāha*) of special (*vi*) responsibilities of household duties. The *gṛhasthāśrama* (household life) starts with the advent of marriage. This *āśrama* is considered the most important as it is connected with *pañca-mahāyajña*s (daily duties) and three great *ṛṇa*s (obligations) further it gives the opportunity to attain three major *puruṣārtha*s: *dharma*, *artha* and *kāma* simultaneously. That is why Manu says it is the real *āśrama* and other ones are either preparatory to this or further development of this *āśrama*. Since *gṛhasthāśrama* starts with the marriage, the wife is considered as the miniature of house itself. The *Mahābhārata* says: "A house without wife is like a forest."

न गृहं गृहमित्याहुः गृहिणी गृहर्मुच्यते।
गृहं तु गृहिणी हीनं अरण्य सदृशंमतम्।।[21]

19. I.P. Desai, "The Joint Family in India", *Sociological Bulletin*, vol. II.

20. H. Nadim, *Samakālīna Bhāratīya Samāja*, Lucknow: Bharat Book Center, 2004, p. 17.

21. *Mahābhārata*, 144.60; also in *Ṛgveda*, 10.86.9 and *Ait. Bra.* 12.5.

na gṛhaṁ gṛhamityāhuḥ gṛhiṇī gṛharmucyate |
gṛhaṁ tu gṛhiṇī hīnaṁ araṇya sadṛśaṁmatam | |

Even in the performance of *yajña*, wife's involvement is essential (यादम्पति समनसा सुनुत — *yādampati samanasā sunuta*)[22] *yajña* always be done with wife (इयं यज्ञं सह पत्नीमिरेत्य — *iyaṁ yajñaṁ saha patnīmiretya*)[23] then only "gods accept it."

In a *yajña* of gods five important functions are necessary. Among them three are to be done with wife:

देवते यज्ञति पञ्च प्रयाजा भविन्त
त्रयोनुयाजाः संयाजयन्ति पत्नीः[24]

devate yajñati pañca prayājā bhavanti |
trayonuyājāḥ saṁyājayanti patnīḥ | |

If someone does it without wife then it will not be a *yajña* (आयज्ञियो वा एषयोऽपत्नीकः — *āyajñiyo vā eṣyo 'patnīkaḥ*)[25] and Vedic sacrifice was compulsion to all the *dvijas*, its absence was considered as great sin. (भुञ्जते ते त्वघं पापा ये पचन्त्यात्मकारणात् — *bhuñjate te tvaghaṁ pāpā ye pacantyātmakāraṇāt*)[26]

The relationship between wife and husband is described as the relationship between river and water or life and body. It is supposed that the wife should always co-operate with her husband till whole life. The wife is also known as *bhāryā* (wife) as her husband takes the responsibility of her livelihood and progeny.

अक्रोधः सत्यवचनं संविभागः क्षमा तथा।

---

22. *Ṛgveda*, 8.31.5.
23. *Atharvaveda*, 19.58.6.
24. *Śatapatha Brāhmaṇa*, 3.1.36.
25. Ibid., 3.7.61.
26. *Bhagavad-Gītā*, 3.13.

प्रजनः स्वेषु दारेषु शौचं अक्रोध एव च।।
आर्जवं भृत्य भरणं नैवेते सार्ववार्णिकः[27]

akrodhaḥ satyavacanaṁ saṁvibhāgaḥ kṣamā tathā | |
prajanaḥ sveṣu dāreṣu śaucaṁ akrodha eva ca | |
ārjavaṁ bhṛtya bharaṇam naivete sārvavārṇikaḥ

Man is considered incomplete without marriage. That is why wife is known as *ardhāṅginī*. As a result of marriage, to fulfil the obligation of ancestors (*pitṝṇa*) the progeny is necessary for them to escape from the hell named as *Put*.[28]

यच्चपुत्रः पुन्नामनरकमनेक शततारं।
तस्यातपातियत्र पुत्रस्य पुत्रत्वम्।।[29]

yaccaputraḥ punnāmanarakamaneka śatatāraṁ |
tasyātapātiyatra putrasya putratvam | |

Atharvaveda says that a son always obeys the orders of his father.

अनुव्रतः पुत्र पुत्री माता भवतु समनः[30]

anuvrataḥ putra putrī mātā bhavatu samanaḥ

The *Bhāgavata* opines that the son who does not adhere to the wishes of his father is just like waste matter (विष्ठा मात्र — *viṣṭhā mātra*).[31]

Change in the Joint Family System

Change is a natural process. It has changed the Indian joint family system from its traditional framework to the modern

---

27. *Mahābhārata*.
28. *Manu*, 9.138.
29. *Gopatha Brāhmaṇa*, 111.12.
30. *Atharvaveda*, 3.30.2.
31. *Śrīmad Bhāgavata*, 9.18.44.

outlook.[32] With the advent of democracy a new ethos has emerged, and individual freedom or independence coupled with individual efforts has taken supreme place in the mind of people. A new rationale has developed to materialize and fulfil the individual happiness. The democratic ethos has caused this change tremendously with the help of newly developed industrialization. Previously it was the agrarian economy which was dependent upon an uncertain monsoon, and likewise it has developed the faith in an uncertain god which created a state of helplessness and dependency on fate. It was converted into the philosophy of extreme satisfaction (सतत् संतुष्टि — *satat saṁtuṣṭi*) at any cost (सन्तुष्टो येन केनचित — *saṁtuṣṭo yena kenacita*)[33] and resistance to change. However, after scientific inventions and the industrial revolution, great changes occurred which influenced the whole societal system. The pattern of education, increase of occupational opportunities, economic affluence, and the newly developed rational scientific approach have started a series of change.[34] Old models were put to examination table, and a new outlook developed under the influence of Western civilization.

The process of Westernization has greatly impacted the traditional Indian family and its values. The new standardization of human activity has led towards cultural manifestations. On the same pedestal, the traditions are also reconstructed or developed in such a way that institutionalization of new value-pattern has become a landmark of new elite culture. Individualism, and a tendency of consumerism are most obvious among such evaluative

32. A.R. Desai, *Rural India in Transition*, Bombay: Popular Book Department, 1967, p. 7.

33. *Bhagavad-Gītā*, 12.14-19.

34. Kingsley Davis, *Human Society*, New York: Macmillan, 1948, p. 470.

changes.[35] The joint family has undergone structural changes in the sense that it is no more thought, compulsory for all the members to live under the same roof or eat from the same kitchen.[36] Due to the compulsion of social mobility, many members migrate to urban centres in search of jobs and better material life, which does have an impact on the earlier sentiment of "jointness" or the "family unity."[37] Only on such important ceremonial occasions as marriages or deaths do the members of the family try to gather together. So it cannot be said that entire sentiment of joint family has become non-existent. But the Westernized mindset and the pattern of education are surely driving this robust Indian social institution towards structural strains.

The traditional approach to life has converted into liberalism, conservative economy has taken shelter in capitalistic framework, and the growing industrial activities have accelerated the process of urbanization. Population growth coupled with family planning has changed the kinship pattern and old lifestyle. Women's education has paved way for their empowerment and individual freedom is considered the supreme goal of life in modern times.

All these factors in conjunction with each other have worked to put pressure on the old Indian joint family system, yet due to its inherent resilience, the institution of joint family has been successfully, resisting many of them, with the result that the primeval sentiment of the joint family system remains intact to a great extent even today.

---

35. Y. Singh, *Social Change in India*, Jaipur: Rawat Publications, 1992, p. 9.
36. S.C. Dube, *Indian Society*, New Delhi: NBT, p. 2.
37. K.M. Panikkar, *Hindu Society at Cross Roads*, Bombay: Asia Publishing House, 1955, p. 7.

7

Family and Women in Vedic Traditions

Divya Tripathi

GṚHASTHĀŚRAMA in today's parlance is called the family life of both man and woman. Woman was considered the backbone of the Vedic society. *Gṛhastha*, amongst all the four *āśrama*s, is considered supreme as it supports the other three. As Manu presents it, the family is the most significant of all social groups. Marriage culminates into family and the child is the central figure of this institution.[1] Even today, we strongly feel that the bringing up of the child, his education, maintenance of social traditions and moulding personality of an individual are mainly connected to the family. The family forms the earliest environment of the child, his first training ground in life; it is the first primary group. Here a child learns about his duties towards parents, brothers, sisters and other relatives. An individual also acquaints himself or herself with ethical and moral values of the society. The family institution, as per Vedic tradition, teaches lessons of selfless service, co-operation, tolerance, love and unselfishness. Many psychologists consider the family as the source of all the charitable tendencies.[2]

1. *Manu-Smṛti*, 9.45.
2. Alwood, *Sociology and Its Psychological Aspects*, p. 213.

Whether the child shall grow up to be a social menace or a well-adjusted individual, with all his faculties functioning at their best, is determined by the family.

During Vedic Age joint family system existed. A joint family has a greater generation depth, i.e. three or four than the nuclear family and the members of which were related to one another by property, income and mutual rights and obligations. Several references prove this. The blessing bestowed upon the couple after the marriage by the *purohita* indicates the above fact. It says:

> May you live here in this house. Do not get separated. Enjoy life by rejoicing and sporting with sons and grandsons, in your own house.[3]

Another *mantra* says:

> Be the mistress of mother-in-law, father-in-law, sister-in-law and brother-in-law.[4]

Manu says of joint family in which all sons of a person live together with their wives and children.[5] Word like *gārgyāyan* in the time of Upaniṣads indicates existence of joint family. Grammatically son of Garga is Gārgeya and son of Gārgeya is Gārgyāyan. These references amply lend credence to the fact that at least four generations stayed together sharing wealth, mutual love and obligations.

Further, even in Pitr̥medha-Sūkta, it is said that oblations were offered to *tāta, tatāmaha, pratatāmaha*.[6] Ghuriya, thus concluded that four generations stayed together in joint family

---

3. *R̥V*, 10.85.42.
4. *AV*, 14.1.44; *R̥V*, 10.85.46.
5. MS, 9.111.
6. *AV*, 18.75-77.

where fourth one knowing his three ancestors, offers them oblations.[7]

Basis of Joint Family

The historical references from Vedas and *Manu-Smṛti* have clearly indicated that ancestor's worship and common property formed the basis of a joint family.

1. ***Śrāddha* (Ancestor's Worship)** — It is the tribute/ respect paid to the memory of ancestors. Ancestor's worship has kept the family members welded together. It was the duty of householder to offer oblations to the "manes" everyday. *Yajurveda* clearly mentioned about the offering of oblations to *pitṛ, pitāmaha, prapitāmaha* for their satisfaction, so that in return, it is believed that they satisfy the householders.[8] Even today these mane's rites are observed twice a year in India.
2. ***Common Property*** — The property right had been the most important common bond of the family. In Vedic tradition, father acted as the head of the family. He was the owner of the property and was responsible for the welfare of the family. It is indicated in *Manu-Smṛti* that the eldest son inherited the ancestral property and younger ones lived under him as they used to be under their father. One of the codes of conduct of the family was that they all had to stay together.[9]

Family Social Relations

The psychological bond between the members of the joint family was so strong that it was put above all other relationship

---

7. G.G. Ghuriya, *Family & Kin*, p. 45.
8. *Yajurveda*,19.36-37.
9. *MS*, 9.105.

in loyalty and support. Thus, there was no sense of insecurity amongst children, women and old people as is clearly visible in modern times. Certain vital social relations in the joint family were between husband and wife, father and son, parents-in-law and daughter-in-law, children and parents, siblings, sister-in-law and brothers' wives.

HUSBAND AND WIFE

Husband and wife together formed the nucleus of the family. In fact, the bride was symbolized as the house.[10] Manu declares.

> The wife is verily the home.

Mahābhārata also declares,

> The house is not the home; the mistress of the house is called the home.

She was regarded as companion as is clear from the *Āpastamba Mantra Brahmaṇ* 1.13.14 where she was addressed as friend. The *Atharvaveda* denotes married woman as a *śakti*; *R̥gveda* as "earth." Correspondingly husband as *prāṇa, Sāmaveda* as heaven (*dyuloka*).[11] And thus, husband-wife were identified as complementary to each other. Man was considered incomplete without woman.[12] So, Gods were prayed to make them and their thinking one.[13]

PARENTS-IN-LAW AND DAUGHTER-IN-LAW

In Vedic tradition bride is welcomed after marriage as queen of the house. During marriage rituals, she was advised to stay with parents-in-law, sister-in-law and brothers-in-law besides

---

10. *jāyedastaṁ maghavan tsedu yoni*. — *R̥gveda*, III.53-4.
11. *AV*, 14.2.71.
12. *Śatapatha Brāhmaṇa*, 5.2.1.10.
13. *R̥gveda*, X.85.46.

husband[14] and behave as mistress looking after them. She took over reins of household management from elders immediately after marriage and shouldered responsibilities of the household like ocean assimilates the several rivers in it[15] and bear their burden.

CHILDREN AND FAMILY

In Vedic joint family system children were looked after by parents and grandparents with love and care.[16] Joint family system provided complete sense of security, emotional and psychological needs that helped in proper development of child's personality. The child observed elder members of the family performing different duties towards others in joint family and subconsciously imbibed virtues like patience and tolerance, sense of service to others, self-sacrifice, endurance, love, respect for elders, and so on and so forth. Joint family system, thus, provided a meaningful education to children and helped developing a virtuous individual of society.

PARENTS AND SON/DAUGHTER RELATIONSHIP

The place of parents was high in a joint family. Mother and father were considered as gods in Vedic texts.[17] Mother was considered most respectable.[18] Vedas described duty of son by saying that son should work according to father's wish and respect the feelings of mother.[19] At the same time, father was required to fulfil his obligations of doing well to his

---

14. *AV*, 14.1.44.
15. *yathā sindhunadīnāṁ sāmrājyaṁ suṣuvevṛṣā* ।
    evā tvaṁ samrājñyedhi patyurastaṁ paretya ॥ — *AV*, 14.1.43
16. *krīḍantau putrarnṛptṛbhiḥ modamānau svegṛhe* । — *ṚV*, 10.85.42
17. *mātṛ devo bhava, pitṛ devo bhava* । — *Taittirīyopaniṣad*, 11.2
18. *sahasraṁ tu pitṛnmātā gauraveṇātiricyate* । — *MS*, 2.145
19. *anuvrataḥ pitu putro mātrā bhavatu saṁmanāḥ* । — *AV*, 3.30.2

children,[20] as an ordained duty. Parents should speak sweetly and support the children in time of crisis[21] as per *Ṛgveda*.

Factors Affecting the Traditional Family System

Fresh economic, social, political and legal factors brought about changes in joint family system. Certain features of the modern era like secularization, industrialization, urbanization, and changed pattern of occupation and job mobility are the few important factors responsible for producing strains in the traditional joint family system. Individuals living in joint households had different conceptions, ideas and also the expectations creating the system of nucleus family. In many cases, individuals live in nuclear households because of social and economic imperatives, yet they follow the joint family norms even today. Nucleus families often meet on social occasions sharing emotional ties even though they live separately. The acceptance of a nuclear family by individuals living in joint households is a clear departure from the norms of the joint family system.

The changing pattern of the traditional family system fulfilled the materialist aspirations of the individuals but did create a situation wherein the basic foundation of learning values, moral and ethical code of conduct or standards, peaceful coexistence and feelings of sharing joy and sorrow could not be kept intact. The individuals in this kind of environment grew as selfish individuals least caring for the feelings and sentiments of others. The Hindu idea/concept of traditional family system not only provided value-based education and social relations but also provided the medium

---

20. *iha te prajāyai priyaṁ smṛdhyatāmatha asmin gṛhe gārhapatyāya jāgṛhi* ।
—*AV*, 14.1.21

21. *pitā mātā madhuvacaḥ suhastā* ।
bhare bhare no yaśasāvaviṣṭhām ॥ — *ṚV*, IV.43.2

for transferring these values from generation to generation for creation of suitable intellectual and social conditions conducive to the smooth functioning of the society.

A proper social order existed for a long time despite many invasions. Despite prolonged political and cultural invasions, true peace and harmony prevailed in the society. When we go deep into the reasons, it was established that intact joint family system was the sole factor responsible for perpetuating the rich cultural legacy of Vedic Era from generation to generation which helped in maintaining a proper social order till recent past.

Woman was the key figure of joint family system occupying the highest pedestal. She contributed immensely in shaping the intellectual and social order of the family and ultimately the society. In fact, it was the woman in every family who inculcated values in the progeny and evolved a happy and peaceful home.

Having thrown some light on traditional Vedic joint family system, it would be worth knowing the status of women in that era that played a prominent role in building up a perfect order in the joint family system. The role and the status assigned to a woman in the Vedic period was highly dignified, positive and constructive, healthy and balanced. In fact, the Vedic philosophy doesn't conceive of any kind of disparity between man and woman. There are no traces of the seclusion of women in Vedic society. Participation of the scholars like Gārgī and Maitreyī in mixed public debates would certify non-existence of the segregation of the women; in fact, this substantiates the fact that Vedic women were highly enlightened.

POSITION AS DAUGHTER

The position of women in the Vedic period can be judged by

the way in which the birth of a girl was received. None of the hymns in *Ṛgveda* considered the birth of a daughter as inauspicious. In fact, there were prayers to get children irrespective of the gender.[22] Though, we find a few *mantras* for the birth of a son in *Atharvaveda* like

> The birth of a girl, grant it elsewhere, here grant a son.[23]

There were some parents who used to perform *kanyā-śrāddha* on the second day of the full moon, for getting a learned and capable daughter.[24] *Ṛgveda* praises the father of many daughters.

Up to 700 BCE initiation of girls was common. They were educated like boys. The *Atharvaveda* observes how a bride had no chance of a good match if she had not been educated as *brahmacāriṇī*. They also had the right to perform the Vedic rituals by themselves.[25] There were as many as 20 learned women,[26] like Lopāmudrā, Ghoṣā and Śulbhā, who had composed many Vedic hymns. Some, like Maitreyī and Gārgī, participated in intellectual and philosophical debates/deliberations.

POSITION AS WIFE

The family life in the Vedic Age was considered to be based on the spiritual relationship of two individuals, who had to perform their duties together towards the society, ancestors, gods and had to march together for their eternal progress. No ceremony was considered effective and complete without her participation.[27] The seer Atri expressly tells Agni:

---

22. *ṚV*, 10.85.38.
23. *AV*, 6.2-3.
24. *Bṛhadāraṇyakopaniṣad*, 4.4.18.
25. *ṚV*, 8.91.1.
26. *Bṛhaddevatā*, 2.82.
27. *Śatapatha Brāhmaṇa*, 5.1.6.10.

> Married pairs, worn out by devout rights, jointly offer abundant sacrificial food, Agni, to thee who art mighty.[28]

The Ṛgvedic hymns speak feelingly of the couple who are united in mind and the gods are invoked to shower their blessings on such a pair as they make their offerings to the gods together.[29] The position of the wife in that age was, therefore, very high.

It is clearly indicated that

> Where the women are honoured, there dwells the gods; but when they are neglected, all religious actions bring no good fruit.
>
> Where women grieve, that family perishes quickly, but where they do not, it prospers.
>
> Houses in which ill-treated women pronounce a curse, perish as if by magic.[30]

Thus, woman was considered as an instrument of prosperity and she deserved honour and recognition from all. Dharmaśāstra in this regard clearly states that women must be honoured and adorned by father, brothers, husband and also by brothers-in-law for their own progress, well-being and prosperity (*MS* 3.55).

POSITION AS MOTHER

In Vedic Age, women held a far more venerable position as a mother than a man as father as is mentioned in the *Gautama Dharma-Sūtra* quoting Vasiṣṭha that:

> The teacher of the Vedas is ten times more venerable than

---

28. *ṚV*, 5.43.15.
29. *ṚV*, 4.58.8
30 *MS*. 3.56-58

> an ordinary teacher; father hundred times a teacher of Vedas and a mother thousand times a father.[31]

Thus, she has been placed above father and teacher out of veneration — this has been rightly said in Upaniṣad as *mātṛ devo bhava*[32] (mother is God).

The educative influence of mother during early years of child is considered incalculable as she was the first teacher of the child in the true sense.

Cormank asserts —

> Traditional India has always accorded women a high place and indeed equality.[33]

There are sufficient references to prove this. In the marriage rituals after pacing the seven steps together, the bridegroom addresses the bride:

> With seven steps, we have become friends,
> May I attain thy friendship,
> May I never fall off from thy friendship,
> May thou never fall off from my friendship,
> Let us combine and harmonize together,
> Let us resolve together that bound in love,
> And ever radiant in each other's company,
> Sharing together all enjoyments and pleasures,
> We may unite our thoughts, duties and our ideals.[34]

Throughout this verse, the stress is laid on equality and friendship between the husband and wife.

---

31. *GDS*, 1.2.56.
32. *Taittirīya Saṁhitā*, 11.2.
33. *She Who Kids a Peacock*, Asia Publishing House 1961 p. 104.
34. *Āpastamba Mantra Brāhmaṇa*, 1.3.14.

The term *dampati*[35] would suggest that the husband and wife were regarded as the joint heads of the household. In one *mantra*, the wife is declared to be half the body of her husband, equally sharing the outcome of good and evil acts. There was perfect parity between the two as is expressed in a Vedic prayer where oneness of hearts is sought between the husband and wife.[36]

It is said that women in ancient India were never regarded as men's equal. The question requires to be examined with care in the correct perspective. Equality as understood in the West means an equality of rights for demanding opportunities for material comforts and gains and recognition. Certainly in this sense it has no place in the Indian thought, where life is meant for spiritual upliftment through duties and not through rights. The Indian sages do not discuss equality of duties for all persons irrespective of inherent differences because of its impossibility in the family, society or the nation. The scheme of duties as enjoined by *dharma* is based on inherent differences in men and women. So, we cannot insist on an equality of duties for all persons in the family. We cannot have it even today.

The requirements for the attainment of the goal of life are adjusted to the nature of the duties one has to perform in life.

The growing demand of gender equality in present times has culminated into a woman liberation movement and is compared by some as Vedic feminism. The society as a whole has given adequate thrust towards total women liberation giving them equal rights and opportunities in every sphere of our social life. However, like their counterpart, a section of women society in their march towards equality in modern

35. *Atharvaveda*, 14.2.64.

36. *R̥gveda*, 10.85.47.

India have construed certain activities like visiting late-night clubs, consumption of alcohol, picking up jobs for economic independence, etc. as an expression of equality. In the bargain what have we achieved? We have created social distress, unhappy homes, shattered families, marital disputes, and emotional and psychological disorders in children. This distorted version of gender equality has affected every segment of our society irrespective of age group over a period of time.

What is important is that the tasks assigned to men are considered more prestigious in most communities and regions. Women's contribution to household is not acknowledged, with the result women are not regarded economically productive. So they are taking up jobs at the cost of family. No doubt this gives economic security but in the bargain she is unable to give greater care and attention to children at home. It hampers the overall development of children. Materialistic glitter is not very important. In the formative years of children, emotional security is essential. Motherly care inculcates virtues of love, patience, and service in the child. So her role as mother and wife should be viewed highly. The rearing of children and household management should be considered equally important by the society.

The exemplary qualities of Indian women like patience, endurance, love, affection, sympathy and tolerance have always been the basis of peace and harmony in the family. Society should realize that these virtues are their strength not weaknesses.

A woman is a mother of race and is liaison between generations. Woman is naturally endowed with the qualities of patience, endurance, affection, sympathy and tolerance. Once she is enlightened, the family is enlightened, the village is enlightened, and the nation is enlightened. To awaken people it is the women who must be awakened. Awakening means a value-based awakening.

The Vedic view of a woman is not to be regarded something as a subject of the past but to be accepted and taken as a blueprint for developing an ideal social structure. As per Vedas, a woman was primarily associated with home and was expected to look after domestic and religious chores. Essentially her role was that of a housewife, a daughter-in-law and mother. She was regarded as *sahadharmiṇī,* a true companion of man in terms of duties and recognition.[37] She has special responsibilities and duties. As the bearing and rearing of children[38] took a good deal of their time and attention, therefore, they were relieved of the economic responsibilities of the family. But the woman in modern era does not respect her own individuality and uniqueness and therefore paying an unconscious tribute to man by trying to imitate him. She is fast becoming masculine and mechanical leading her into a kind of conflict with her own innate nature.

Let family unit be strong, let there be women like Sītā and Sāvitrī, let every woman become Jījābāī for imparting moral education to children through stories and their own character; let there be more men like Lincoln to proclaim that —

> What I am and what I long to be, the credit of all this goes to my mother.

---

37. *R̥V*, X.85.47.

38. *MS*, 9.28.

8

Cultural and Ritualistic Traditions of Indian Family*

Rabi N. Mishra

INDIAN family tree is the proverbial banyan tree, nourished by mutual love and infinite sacrifice. It vows to provide shade to everyone even while burning itself. It reflects "Unity in Diversity" as it embraces the concept of *kuṭumba,* all the near and dear ones represented by a common thread of *gotra*. The love for a fellow being starts when the foetus is in the womb and lingers even after the lifeless body is consigned to the "undefined world." With the symptoms of pregnancy, the welcome ceremony begins. Utmost care is taken of the mother, as she carries the chariot of the new guest to the family of human race. *Goda Bharāī* (carrying of the child) is conducted by inviting all friends and relatives in which a sweet sense is given to the child on what it means to be a human being. That selfless love and mutual fellow-feeling is the fundamental tenet of a human being is thus inculcated at the most primary state. It is also ensured that the child remains both physically and ethically healthy by way of the mother being fed with both sāttvic food and soothsayings. A pregnant woman is seen as a good omen as a mark of respect to the incoming member of

* Inputs provided by Kamala Mishra are lovingly acknowledged.

the family. She is loved and well-treated so that the new arrival learns love and affection from the very beginning. That an unborn child also tends to learn has been narrated in the *Mahābhārata,* wherein Arjuna's son Abhimanyu is said to have learnt the art of breaking the *cakravyūha* as he heard it from his father telling his mother even while he was in his mother's womb. As the child arrives with a loving cry, the sign of apprehension as it lands in an unknown land, the boundless care of the hosts around transforms that into a sweet smile, the sign of relief that he is in safe hands. A set of celebration then follows. A child in a family, as the revered guest, is treated as the God incarnate and is showered with love by one and all in the community. Thus the lesson of "to treat humans as humans," the fundamental *dharma* of human race begins in an Indian family from as early as the time of conception in the mother's womb.

In the family, the relationship-salutations are conducive to germination of a serious sense of fellow-feeling. All the seniors of the father are called as "senior father" and the seniors of the mother are "senior mother." The respective younger relatives are called as "junior father" and "junior mother." Their children are then taken to be loved as brothers and sisters. This way, the child gets the scope of learning to respect elders as own parents, while getting trained to share possessions with a bunch of brothers and sisters. In a pool of near and dear ones around, the child gets trained to "live and let live." In a typical Indian joint family (which is showing the signs of disintegration) everyone is treated equally, irrespective of the quantum of contribution to the earnings pool. All the earning units deposit their earnings into a corpus under the custody of the eldest of the family. He then allocates the resources to their optimum use for the overall benefit of the whole family while taking care that everyone's genuine needs are adequately met. This sort of practice of managing a household as a compact economic unit run on optimal commercial lines generates a sense of responsibility and tolerance in the minds of each of the members. The distinct nature of a typical "Indian" embodies all these virtues.

There has been a grievance that such family units are run autocratically by the eldest.

This may not be true.

(a) *yuktiyuktam vaco gr̥hyam; bālādapi, śukādapi*
yuktiyuktam vaco sthajyam; vr̥dhādapi, śukādapi

If the submissions of a child or even a parrot are logical, those should be accepted, while the same of an old man may be rejected.

(b) *mā karo dhana, jana, yauvana garvam.*

One must not show off wealth, servants/followers and youth.

(c) *agādha jala sañcārī, rohito naiva garvitaḥ*
ganduṣa jala mātrena safari farfarāyate

In the deepest down the river, Rehu, the king of fish enjoys remaining to itself. But, in the bank of the river, in a small patch of water, Safari; the tiny/bony fish makes lot of noise attracting public attention.

(d) *namrate falino vr̥kṣa, namrate guniṇo janaḥ.*

A tree laden with fruits and a human with knowledge is bound to be polite.

(e) *akr̥tyam naivya kartavyam, prāṇatyāgepi saṁsthite*
na ca kr̥tye parityajyam, eṣa dharma sanātanams

You must carry out what you consider is your duty and ignore what is not.

Such ideas having being included in the lullaby of the family elders and the syllabus of Indian schools, speak highly of the moral standards every Indian family member is supposed to be ornamented with. Respecting elders does not mean remaining subservient to unacceptable ideas. Nor knowledge/ education directs disrespect to the unlettered elders. Indian family allows space for everyone. A sweet blend of knowledge, experience and practical know-how makes each family member more matured and enlightened to face the vicissitudes of life. The project of *sāgara-manthana* or the churning of the Milky Ocean, another tale from the grandma's ocean of love speaks of the virtues of division of labour in a family set-up for optimum utilization of available resources. Both the gods from the state of heaven and the satans from the state of hell (together forming the family of the universe) were persuaded by the supreme office of Nārāyaṇa to churn the sea. Everyone lent his hand. The products procured, namely, the Kāmadhenu (the wish-fulfilling cow), the Ucchaiśravas (the flying horse), the Airāvata (white elephant of great beauty), the *kaustubha maṇi* (a priceless jewel), Lakṣmī (the Goddess of Wealth) and finally, *amṛta* (the nectar of immortality), were distributed to everyone as per their contribution and eligibility.

The Indian culture remains hinged on the concept of *vasudhaivakuṭumbakam*: "the whole universe is a close-knit joint-family." The micro pervades into the macro. The sense of fellow-feeling, the idea of sharing with others whatever little one has, takes the roots in a family set-up and in due course gets entangled in each member's mind and the feeling of "family membership" spreads. This was not just a religious rhetoric. That this idea was deeply ingrained in the Indian mind is reflected in the writings of a poor, blind, little-educated tribal poet from an interior corner of the state of Orissa, Bhīmā Bhoi, by name. As is obvious, though, he had enough of human misery, while lamenting the intensity of poverty all around, was praying to God for the restoration of human dignity in exchange for his deportation to even hell. Sans the power of vision, he was able to see the maladministration in the kingdom of mankind and was seeking illumination of the human mind. This is in line with what Vedas had to say: "Let there be balance in everything; Let there be peace and peace; let such peace be with everyone of us."

The new member of the family, while completing her voyage from the womb to the world, greets the other members with hands folded and head down. Indian family traditions define this act in this way. It means that everyone ought to bow down before the God within the other. God lives in every human soul and lives on love and sacrifice. He who serves fellow beings is deemed to have served God. *Mānava sevā* is *mādhava sevā*. By so doing the new member comes with a vow to serve the mankind. Folding of hands reflects: "you and me : a cup of love in-between" and by so doing an eternal source of love is brought in-between him and the other members of the family who reciprocate in the same way by laying themselves down and drowning him into their heart and soul. A saga of love thus begins. This flow of love never stops even near the grave. While leaving this earthly body, the family member gets the same kind of salutation. He is decorated with all that he liked during his lifetime and given a send-off by all whom he loved or loathed. He comes with the message of love and departs with malice to none. As the Lord Himself claims in the *Bhagavad-Gītā*, the trip from one "cradle to grave" gets just transformed into another. That is why the rituals of feast, decoration, and family get-together are common for both when a member arrives and when he takes his leave.

The grin, with which she comes in, turns into smile getting infested with smiles all around. Heart is the dividing wall between a grin and a smile. Sans the involvement of the heart, the beholder sees the smile as a grin. Smile is the most infectious. A smile rarely remains unreciprocated. That is why the smile of the newcomer spreads smile all over. Indian family set-up has smile and reverence (*namaste* with folded hands) as its backbone. It is said that smile requires only four muscles whereas grin/frown requires sixteen. Then why waste the use of twelve muscles? If we do so, overuse of muscles may stiffen them resulting in *smile* turning automatically into a *grin*. Sri Sri Ravishankar says, "a child smiles four hundred times a day, an adolescent only seventeen times and an adult does not smile at all. And that too, if he becomes a little successful, he becomes much more stiff."

To appreciate the essence of an Indian family, the most appropriate example could be that of Lord Śiva, the destroyer of what is inappropriate. The inmates there are He Himself, Mātā Pārvatī, His wife, and their two sons, Gaṇeśa and Kārttikeya. The support staffs are: the snake (adorning His neck), the bull (His *vāhana*), the peacock (Kārttikeya's *vāhana*), the rat (Gaṇeśa's *vāhana*) and the lion (Pārvatī's *vāhana*). The relationship between lion and bull, snake and peacock and rat are well known. Although they are inherently after each other's life, they hardly ever fight even while living under one roof. A sense of absolute loyalty and dedicated love for their masters keep them balanced enough to forget even their natural instinct. This testifies to the fact that absolute surrender to the cause of mutual trust and fellow feeling is the best bet for a purposeful life. This idea develops adequately in the green pastures of an Indian family environment and has the potentials for spreading all over. Śravaṇa Kumāra gave his life for his blind parents. Rāma sacrificed his royal kingdom happily to ensure that his father's words are respected. Lakṣmaṇa and Bharata embraced *vanavāsa suo motu* following in the footsteps

9a - Rabi Mishra, presenting his paper

9 - Rabi Mishra (standing), Visiting Faculty, Harvard University

of their brother. Such was the intensity of the bondage of love in an Indian family!

rahimana dhāgā prema kā, mata toṛo caṭkāye ।
ṭūṭe se phir nā juḍe, juḍe gāṇṭha paṛa jāye ॥

Never break the thread of love. It cannot be joined back without a knot.

The Indian culture also hinges on the philosophy of "give, give and give." The parents help the children till they are capable of standing on their own feet. The elder helps the younger and so on till all the children are on their own. To give them emotional support marriages are organized as a common family effort. As per Indian family practice one cannot get his debts written off even at death. His offsprings have to repay it. This means that one should try always to remain in credit in his personal account. Harming someone would invite a debit entry while helping someone would invite a credit entry. In order hence to remain in net credit, one has to have the habit of helping others. Help need not only be in material terms. The easiest and costless way of remaining in net credit would be to develop the habit of showing reverence with folded hands and with a smile. Learning to smile away makes life easier to live. Indian family teaches this simple philosophy throughout. This also indicates the virtue of gratefulness as a necessary by-product of Indian family life. The contributions of the elders in the family are revered and well remembered by the younger ones. This prompts them to look after them in their old-age and even after their death in terms of various rituals of love and care as narrated elsewhere.

Giving and getting are in fact the two sides of the same coin. This is backed by a natural law that wealth always comes back tenfold to the person who gives. If one opts out of linking wealth only to the stock of material money/assets, "giving" has nothing to do with parting of one's surplus stock of money/assets, an act, which exclude people having less/ insufficient of them. If we include "character," "ethical values," "knowledge of self-cure," etc. as part of wealth as well, everyone in the society gets a viability to "give" to someone else. This kind of thinking for mankind is beyond the horizon of classical/neoclassical economics of nationalism, while it bodes well for the modern concept of the economics of globalization. Here one emulates sans the aim to dominate. Quality of giving could be a dominant variable for wealth creation for economic growth and distribution, a facet of economics; it is high time modern economists dared to experiment seriously. As such, it is a part of the Indian culture to donate Rs. 101 instead of Rs. 100 or Rs. 1001 instead of Rs. 1000. It is believed that it fosters an intention to keep giving in future also (Swami Tejomayananda). Further, that one extra rupee also signifies that one should always give a little more than what is expected, as also a little more than what needs to give or share. Sharing of consumer surplus as a matter of mental bend is the focus. It does not presuppose subventing lack of effort or inertia to imitate or emulate. It is just a commitment to the society, of "giving more than what we take" and "producing more than what we consume." It is economic-status-neutral. It is wealth ownership-neutral as well. As per Upaniṣads, the whole universe is a divine endowment, in which one should enjoy one's rightful share without a false sense of possession, and without depriving others of their legitimate due. The mediating mechanism for this complex distribution process is not an "invisible" market system, but mature self-restraint exercised by people in the overall interest of the system. Gandhian concept of *sarvodaya* revolves around this idea, the "development of all." It is very interesting to observe certain typical Indian habits. These are still prevalent across all the states. Food in the household is taken only after a small portion is offered to "cow," "dog," "crow" and the place of worship for the "hungry." In most of the religious celebrations, one portion of food is offered to the "ancestors." It may appear on the surface superstitious or foolish but one needs to go into its logic. Sharing of whatever little one has with everyone around brings peace and harmony. It goes with the saying that an island of poverty is a threat to prosperity everywhere. Offerings to those whom one owes his existence, God and ancestors displays the virtue of "gratefulness," which, in fact, automatically kills one other vice, "vindictiveness" and encourages one, "forgiveness." Indian family rituals of *śrāddha* ceremony is an excellent example of how such virtues could be practised. On the day of *Mahālaya,* in a day long rigorous worship, ancestors of the last seven lives are called upon to come (by reciting their names) and have the food of their choice. A joint prayer is organized for their comforts even in their heavenly abode. Thus, appreciating the hardship of fellowmen and even those who are not alive is a great lesson learnt from such customs. Glorifying the virtuous and vilifying the evil are the fundamental teachings of some of the regular annual Indian family functions, namely Dusserah, Dīpāvalī, Holī, etc. These celebrations leave a mark in the memory of the family members since their childhood not to fall prey to envy, selfishness and greediness for others' wealth.

Indian culture gives primary importance to dignity of women. "Mātr̥śakti" (the power of women or Mother) is considered as the ultimate source of strength. Goddess Durgā, Kālī, Santoṣī Mātā are symbolic of the helplessness of even gods in containing the Satans, as they were specifically created and empowered by the combined forces of the entire God-kingdom. And the forces of evil were trounced. One does not get any benefit of a visit to any temple of a God without following it up with the same of His Goddess wife. Lord Jagannātha (at Purī in the state of Orissa) during the famous car festival visits Guṇḍīca (the abode of a queen who supervised the making of His idolic form) and makes it a point to take sister Subhadrā along. The aura of Lord Jagannātha's temple is universally scented with the fragrance of the presence of temples of Mā Vimalā and Mā Lakṣmī in the same compound. The positive contribution of women to economic prosperity has since been empirically tested. Study on women in Asia and Africa has indicated that investment on women empowerment by way of increased health care and education fetches better results on wealth creation compared to those on men. As mother they nourish and enable, as sister they love and respect, and as wife they share and resurrect. They are half the productive powers but for which potentials for growth cannot be harnessed to the full. They bear the torch for the home and the society. Ignoring them would mean losing the torch and inviting darkness.

Commercialization of mind is creating a sense of self-induced amnesia about the values a traditional Indian family endows one with. The missing link between generational wavelengths is growing. The ethical *mantras* are no longer being whispered into the ears of the new-borns in the family leading to breaking of the chain of the channel of communication between various spaces of time. The new generation is getting excited about what is *novel* (not necessarily *noble*) in the Western world, thus tending to lose the *dharma* of an Indian, i.e. to treat a human being like a human being and not a commodity.

Indian family system is on the crossroads, so are the family members. Children are slowly drifting apart from the elders.

Old-age homes are coming up very fast. *Money* is trying to outpace *love* as the means to satisfy the duty towards the elders. Mutual trust is crumbling. The arrogance of knowledge is tending to threaten the paternal authority of love and goodwill as authoritarian and blind.

The only way to find the right path would be to go back to the basics . . . sit near the grandfathers/mothers . . . remember and relearn the ethics of Indian family system.

If we opt to remember the mornings in an Indian family or an Indian school, we can hear the fragrance of the past . . .

> *sarve bhavantu sukhinaḥ*
> *sarve santu nirāmayaḥ* ।
> *sarve bhadrāṇi paśyantu*
> *mā kaścit duḥkha bhāva bhavet* ॥

Let us recall grandpa's quotation from the *Bhagavad-Gītā*; what Lord Kṛṣṇa says to Arjuna on what should be the attitude for the ultimate in life.

> What has happened has happened for the best. What is happening is happening for the best. What will happen will happen for the best. Do not brood over the past. Do not worry about the future. The present is on. What have you lost that you are weeping? What have you brought that you have lost? What have you made that have been destroyed? You brought not anything. What you have you got from here. What was given here. What you took you took from the universe. What you gave, you gave to this universe.You have come empty-handed and shall go empty-handed. What is yours today, was somebody else's in the past and will be somebody else's in the future. You think it is yours and deeply engrossed in it. This attachment is the cause of all your sorrow. Change is the law of nature. What you call death is life itself. In a moment you are a millionnaire, in the very next you are a poor man. Mine, yours, small, big, ours,

> theirs; remove this from your mind, then everybody is yours and you are everybody's.

Everyone came to this world naked and will leave it in the form of ashes. Then on what rational basis can anyone claim universal ownership of the bounty of nature? A piece of paper should not be enough to justify the entitlement over material possessions which someone has snatched away from other fellow human beings by virtue of their helplessness or otherwise. The power to enjoy public wealth should come only from the "permit" issued by God, the owner and custodian of this land called Universe.

This has been the cornerstone of Indian culture firmly laid on a sweet family structure. We ought not allow it to die a premature death.

9

The Wealth of Joint Families

Mona Khaitan

Empirical evidence suggests that the number of traditional joint families amongst Indians is on the decline while nuclear families are on the rise. The paper emphasizes the importance of joint families as a vehicle for accumulating wealth, both material and relational. While material wealth provides material goods and services, the relational wealth provides a sense of belonging and fulfilment, satisfying a deep inner urge for wholeness. Material wealth may be changed to amass relational wealth. Relational wealth fosters individual harmonious growth, by purifying the mind to know the Self. Knowledge of Self is liberation from the cycle of rebirths. Thus, the relational wealth constitutes the real wealth of joint families.

विहाय कामान् यः सर्वान् पुमांश्चरति निःस्पृहः ।
निर्ममो निरहंकारः स शान्तिम् अधिगच्छति ।।२.७१।।

vihāya kāmān yaḥ sarvān pumaṁścarati niḥspṛhaḥ ।
nirmamo nirahaṁkāraḥ sa śāntim adhigacchati ॥ 2.71 ॥

One who abandons all desires and becomes free from longing and the feeling of "I" and "my" attains peace.

— *BG*. 2.71

THESE are heady days for India and her people. Economic growth with its accompanying dizzying GDP numbers is displayed everywhere. Indeed, as the Western world admires and claps, the Indians experience a sense of bewilderment along with uneasy elation. They think, "yes, we are doing excellent work — look at these astounding numbers." (see Appendix 1) Obviously, Indians deserve an overdue acknowledgement and recognition for who they are. There is a renewed sense of pride. Some have participated in this economic prosperity directly and benefited by acquiring more material goods, a common indicator of standard of living. However, the majority are yet to see this prosperity trickle down but have participated vicariously by being merely associated with India.

As this economic boom progresses and carries all forward of its own momentum, it is time to pause to reflect if this is where India should be going. What is likely to be the outcome of this so-called Western economic progress in India? Is it what the Indian and/or the global community really want? Would this bring happiness or misery in its wake? Most fortunately, we have a living laboratory in the Western world where this run after material wealth has yielded very little in terms of individual happiness and many problems that have become entrenched. The biggest ailment is the break-up of the family as a result of the pressures being put on it. Indeed, the nuclear families of the Western world are breaking up with more households headed by single parents.[1] Moreover, divorces are on the rise, teenage pregnancies are common, and crime and drug use are escalating at alarming rates. Most urban areas are crime-sinfested, so a typical American seeking safety has moved to the suburbs. Even here, he[2] does not feel

1. Data is for 2004-05, unless specified otherwise.
2. India's ranking, where applicable, are specified in brackets, linked to the source data.

10 - Mona Khaitan, MassBay Community College

10a - Mona Khaitan, presenting her paper

safe, so lives in gated communities. In other words, the average affluent citizen has become a prisoner who, instead of being able to roam at liberty, lives in walls of his own making. Romesh Diwan, an eminent Professor of Economics at Rensselaer Polytechnic Institute, attributes the deterioration in the general quality of life to be related to (1) income distribution, (2) anxiety, (3) overconsumption, and (4). community (*Relational Wealth*, 307). In his estimation, the breakdown of the family, and in turn the community, is responsible for the worsening of the quality of life. The lesson to be learned from this live laboratory is to ensure that the families, specifically the traditional joint families, remain strong in India and not be allowed to deteriorate into nuclear or broken nuclear families. There appears to be much debate over whether the joint families are disappearing and being replaced by nuclear families as a consequence of industrialization and the subsequent urbanization in India (Agarwala, 1962; Cohen 1981, cited in Niranjan, Nair, and Roy 623). In a socio-economic analysis of the size and structure of the family in India, the researchers conclude that "empirical evidence in this study also supports the fact that the joint family system is continuing but in considerably lower percentages when compared to nuclear families. Over the years, the proportion of nuclear families has shown a significant increase" (ibid., 628). This article proposes that relational wealth is the only real wealth and acquired more readily in a joint family than in a nuclear family structure.

Definition of a Joint Family

For our purposes, the joint family includes both the lineally extended and collaterally extended families as well as supplemented nuclear families and supplemented broken nuclear families (see Appendix 2). The joint family definition ncludes families that are geographically dispersed for business 'easons, but stay connected socially and emotionally. A family ›perating a unit of business in the United States, while the 'est of the family resides in different areas of the world, 'emains a joint family. Clearly, with improved communication, he ability to stay connected has become easier, presenting an ›pportunity for far-flung members to stay emotionally and ocially attached, despite long distances. One very large family ıas a reunion every month with over 100 households ›articipating in the readily available free conference-calling ɔ stay in touch. Hence, the definition of a joint family is xtended to include supplemented families and geographically ispersed families bonding economically, socially, and motionally. The enormous proportion of joint family ties is ɘflected in the non-resident remittances to India (population .1b) of $10 billion, while Chinese (population 1.3b) non-ɘsident remittances amounted to $1.2 billion in year 2001 Ɔange, Jagannath, and Parajia, *Indians Adrift in China*, 18).

mphasis on Joint Family

his article emphasizes joint families because of the relational yıamics inherent in such families. The joint families are in a nique position to amass both types of wealth: material and lational.

On a continuum, the joint families do better in developing ıd amassing material wealth than nuclear families, with the uclear families faring better than the broken nuclear families ıd singles. When a household operates as a joint family, it ıjoys a higher level of income, owns property, and/or ısiness. From the NFHS[3] data, it is discovered that the income vel of the joint families is relatively higher than that of the ıclear families. The joint family households with low income

3. *Rest of the data* from the World Factbook, dated 1 November 2005.

constitute only 35 per cent of low income households, while nuclear families constitute 65 per cent of low income households. The income of joint family climbs to 49 per cent for medium income households, while nuclear families have a medium income of 51 per cent. The joint families constitute 53 per cent of the total high income households, while the nuclear families constitute 47 per cent of the total high income households. This is while the joint family represents only 42 per cent of the urban households and 46 per cent of rural households (Niranjan, Nair, and Roy, 649-51). This slightly better economic success of the joint family is due to the complex dynamics present in the joint family. Statistically, the probability of a joint family living at low income levels is less than at medium or high income levels in comparison to a nuclear family. This is easily explained. A joint family enjoys economies of scale; the costs are lower than if two or three households were to be maintained, making for increased income.

Relational wealth is a relatively new concept advanced by Diwan (*Relational Wealth*, 319). This is intangible wealth and once amassed promotes the physical, emotional, intellectual, and psychic well-being of each individual. It serves to generate a feeling of connectedness with a firm sense of belonging. Diwan says,

> It is a state in which a person is surrounded only and only by other persons whom s/he cares and who care for this person. The underlying principle is love, caring and sharing. This is in fact an expression of spiritual living. The level of consumption of physical goods is at a minimal. It is a state where people live together in families of blood relations or of friends, where commitments are made and kept, where one's greatest pleasure is to see that the other person is satisfied and happy. — *Gandhian Economics*, 285

In other words, the spiritual living underlying relational wealth advances harmonious spiritual growth of the individual. Diwan further argues that, "the joint (family) living requires not only negotiating skills but a basic capacity for caring, loving, giving and forgiving. It is this capacity to love, to give, and to serve that is necessary for a spiritual life" (ibid., 287). Significantly, Diwan's advocacy of joint family living for creating relational wealth is supported by sociological research.

> Much of the research literature dealing with family life in India recognizes that the joint family is considered to be an ideal type of family and that most Indians, at some point in their lives, participated in joint family living. — Nandan and **amp**; Eames, 1980, qtd. in Medora, Larson, and Dave 408.

The philosophy underlying the concept of relational wealth is the ancient Hindu philosophy that when an individual serves another, he serves and benefits the Whole, which means that the act benefits all including the individual. The *Īśa Upaniṣad* peace invocation speaks of the nature of this universe as being of Fullness (*Brahman*). It is also the true nature of man and the theme of the Upaniṣad is therefore the achievement by man of his true nature, the fullness of his being, *pūrṇatā.* The search of man is the search for fullness, for completeness, for fulfilment, for integrality, for wholeness. This is the highest insuppressible aspiration of man. This is the deepest human yearning and every act of man has fulfilment as his goal, the urge to wholeness for its motive (Ranganathananda, 68). It certainly is not for more refrigerators or dryers or cars or a bigger bank account. In fact, people begin to find that material wealth fails to satisfy after the initial need for minimum food, shelter, and clothing has been met. No physical good can satisfy the intense craving of man for fullness. The place where this fullness can be achieved is in the joint family system or in an *āśrama* (hermitage — often a monastery). In a nuclear family, one acts not for the welfare of others, but for the lower self, as the child or spouse has become an extension of one's ego. That ego is being served. But in the joint family, the relatives lack that extension of ego, providing an opportunity for service. It is neither realistic nor desirable for all persons to lead a monastic life, so the joint family system offers a viable alternative for acquiring relational wealth.

History of Joint Families and Wealth

There is a vast amount of Hindu literature available on efficacy of joint family and the appropriate approach towards wealth. The wealth must be earned by honest means, maintained without hoarding, and distributed to the needy on a regular basis. Possession by one is possession by all. One must not covet another's property as nothing belongs to us. The best way to enjoy wealth is with detachment and a sense of renunciation (*Īśa*. 1).

THE REVERED HISTORY BOOKS: THE RĀMĀYAṆA AND THE MAHĀBHĀRATA

The two great history books written in India both provide a vivid, detailed picture of joint family life during the ancient Indian period prior to 400 BCE. Declared Swami Vivekananda, "In fact, the *Rāmāyaṇa* and the *Mahābhārata* are the two encyclopedias of the ancient Aryan life and wisdom, portraying an ideal civilization, which humanity has yet to aspire after" (97). Sage Vālmīki, the biographer of *Rāmāyaṇa*, related the history of this period in the form of poetry (*kāvya*) comprising 24,000 stanzas, for the benefit and instruction of posterity. This instruction leaves a powerful impression on the reader's mind when the reader realizes that what the *Rāmāyaṇa* teaches, Śrī Rāma and his extended family actually practised and is not a mere precept. Śrī Rāma led an ideal life as an obedient and dutiful son, an affectionate brother, a loving husband, an upholder of *dharma* for the protection of the weak and helpless, and an ideal king. Lakṣmaṇa, Bharata, and Śatrughna were ideal brothers, while Sītā was an ideal wife upholding a wife's duty (*strī-dharma*). The father of Śrī Rāma, Rājā Daśaratha was an ideal father, and the three mothers were ideal mothers of the household. The entire joint family of the four married brothers, given to personal sacrifice and service to others, are perfect role models for any family, and specifically for those in a joint family system. As the *Rāmāyaṇa* is the history of a ruling royal family, it contains lessons in polity, administration, diplomacy, war, and other topics related to governance based on *dharma*. Many precepts related to the proper outlook on sense enjoyment (*kāma*) are found in the context of events of this historic family. The family followed lofty ethical ideals: one should be willing to die to protect one's promise (*raghukula rīti sadā calī āyī; prāṇa jāye para vacana na jāyī*). It was common practice for a king to conduct massive fire sacrifices (*yajña*) at regular intervals, where a large number of people from all walks of life were invited, and honoured with expensive gifts. The best outcome of this festivity was considered to be where the king distributed not only all the wealth he had collected in the form of taxes as sanctioned by the Śāstras, but also the original wealth he had been enjoying. The day after this disbursement of all wealth in the *Aśvamedha Yajña*, Śrī Rāma was left only with earthen pots (De, 37). The wealth (*artha*) is acquired so it affords an ability to give. Thus, in the *Rāmāyaṇa*, the life of Śrī Rāma depicts a perfect balanced ideal of wealth, pleasure, and *dharma*.

The *Mahābhārata* is a unique history book of ancient India. Unique because it is the longest book (100,000 verses) authored by mankind. Unique because it is a history book written in poetry with meticulous sublime verses. Unique because it covers all subjects known to man. It unabashedly states this fact: "Whatever is here may be found elsewhere; but what is not here cannot be found anywhere else" (ibid., 66). Literally, the great history book of the *Mahābhārata* has every topic known to man including how to live in a joint family as well as how not to live in a joint family. It also covers all aspects of wealth, its generation, maintenance, and disposal in great detail. An invaluable part of the *Mahābhārata* is the *Śrīmad Bhagavad-Gītā*, which consists of eighteen chapters (23 to 40) of the Bhīṣma Parva. In it, Śrī Kṛṣṇa teaches Arjuna, the struggling aspirant, the highest philosophy of non-attached selfless actions of *karma-yoga*, the science of action, for attaining peace and tranquillity of mind.

During the *Mahābhārata* period, the four primary caste had come into existence and remained in their pristine form In the Śānti Parva of the *Mahābhārata* (XII.188.10), it states that there is no distinction of caste (*varṇa*), and that the whole of this universe is divine, having emanated from *Brahman* (the Supreme Spirit); created (equally) by *Brahman*; men had, on account of their actions (*karma*) been divided into various castes (ibid., 75). The *Mahābhārata* describes the four aims (*puruṣārtha*) of life to be: duties (*dharma*), generation of wealth (*artha*), enjoyment of sense objects (*kāma*), and liberation (*mokṣa*).

The Dharma-Sūtras and the Dharma-śāstras

While the Vedas explain mainly the two great objectives of human life (*puruṣārtha*), *dharma* and *mokṣa* conceptually, the six Vedāṅgas and the Smṛtis form authoritative sources on *dharma* in practice. One of the Vedāṅgas is *Kalpa-Sūtra*, with three sections called Śrauta, Gṛhya, and Dharma. Of particular interest for our purpose is the Gṛhya-Sūtras that give information on the numerous ceremonies associated with leading a householder's life including the 40 *saṁskāra*s performed at distinct times during the life. The Dharma-Sūtras are connected with Gr̥hya-Sūtras and deal with *dharma,* which means, right, duty, law, religion, custom, and usage (ibid., 301).

The term "Dharmaśāstra" is generally applicable to both the Dharma-Sūtras and the metrical codes, known as Smr̥tis. The *Manu-Smr̥ti* is the most ancient and authoritative work in existence on *dharma*. It has twelve chapters consisting of customs (*ācāra*), conduct (*vyavahāra*), and penance (*prāyaścitta*) for guiding the life of a householder (ibid., 309).

The Vedic seers in the Dharmaśāstras divided the life of each individual into four stages or *āśrama,* literally meaning "to toil," indicating that the Vedic man realized that spiritual progress could only be made through effort. The purpose of the precious human birth is to advance in spiritual growth to eventually liberate oneself from the cycle of rebirths. To this end, the Vedic seers geared all life stages to incrementally purify the mind. In the first student stage of life (*brahmacārin*), a person is required to study to gain knowledge, specifically of *dharma,* one's duties in life. Student life is expected to be a life of chastity and continence. The instruction in the duties and obligations, *dharma,* would help the individual conduct his next householder stage (*gr̥hastha*), where the Vedic seers expanded the aims of life to include generation of wealth (*artha*) as well as enjoyment (*kāma*) of it, always in accordance with *dharma.* The duty of a householder is to support the people in the other three stages of life: students, retired persons or hermits (*vānaprasthī*), and ascetics (*saṁnyāsī*). Once the householder fulfils the duties of the household, then the householder may retire with his spouse. At this point, the retired person leads an austere celibate life of *dharma* with the spouse and foregoes the enjoyment of wealth and sense objects. The objective is to wean and purify the mind slowly in preparation for renunciation. If the householder adopts the last stage of renunciation, then the individual gives up all to lead a solitary life with the sole aim of liberation (*mokṣa*), dedicating time to concentration and meditation, sustaining body for this purpose alone. The joint family is of great value in supporting the members of the family in the other three stages of life. It provides a security net for all members of the family to advance in their spiritual life.

VĀRTĀ AND ARTHAŚĀSTRA

Ancient sages have categorized knowledge or learning (Śāstra or Vidyā) into four distinct branches: philosophy (*aṇvikṣiki*), three Vedas (*trayī*), economics (*vārtā*), and polity (*daṇḍanīti*). *Vārtā* etymologically signifies *vṛtti* or means of livelihood, but is in particular used to denote the *vṛtti* allotted to the vaiśyas (business people). *Vārtā* is also used to denote the study of employment. Kauṭilya, a recognized authority on *Arthaśāstra* and a master of a treatise of 6,000 *śloka*s on *Arthaśāstra* (app. 400-100 BCE) considers *vārtā* to deal with farming, cattle management, and trade. Later additions to the study of *vārtā* include the subjects of banking and industry. *Arthaśāstra*, in its technical sense, covers a wider field than *vārtā* and *daṇḍanīti*, and contains jurisprudence, politics, and economics (ibid., 655). Its scope includes the acquisition and preservation of dominion or art of government in its widest sense of the term (ibid. 451). The sages have recognized the importance of economics to individual's well-being as well as for the stability of the country. The *Arthaśāstra*, the histories, the Smṛtis and other works on ancient Indian economics have understood the importance of wealth in the pursuit of life's fourfold objective (*puruṣārtha*). The Vedic seers have recommended the acquisition of wealth (*artha*) at the householder stage of life (*gṛhastha āśrama*) for leading a life of service and charity.

THIRUKKURAḶ

Thiruvalluvar, a Tamil saint living in app. 200 BCE, is the author of *Thirukkuraḷ*, a succinct ancient Tamil classic textbook on philosophy and ethics consisting of 1,330 couplets (*kuraḷ*s). He diagnoses the human nature with penetrating insight and exceptional skill in poetic form of couplets and has written on virtue (*dharma*), wealth (*artha*), and happiness or love (*kāma*). The final aim of life, *mokṣa* is implied in the three aims of life. This exceptional ethical text is practical as well as idealistic. His suggestions for translating the ideals into action are valuable and conform to modern psychology.

The first part on "virtue" describes a view of life which starts with the natural attachment to the family; but its love gradually passes beyond the narrow bounds through ever-expanding circles of love till it encompasses one's own society. Then begins the blossoming of love into universality.

The householders are the backbone of the society. Families preserve the memory of the past generation and take care of guests, relatives, friends, and themselves as well (*K*, 41-43).[4] Love and virtue should characterize the family life. Love refers to the husband and wife's mutual love, their love for their children and kindness towards all others whom they serve. Virtue refers to the fair and honest means of earning wealth and the family's dealing with the various sections of people. The whole purpose of family life is to discipline the senses and perform various duties virtuously. It was the common practice to divide the income of a family into six parts: one part was for the ruler and the remainder for performing the family's fivefold duty to the ancestors, gods, guests, kindred, and one's own family. In the current age, this would be taxes, offering of food to the departed ancestors (*śrāddha*), taking care of old parents, support of temples and spiritual organizations, entertaining of guests, friends, and relatives.

Guests are different from friends and relatives, being unexpected visitors who come to the door of the house. The householder should shun evil means such as cheating, stealing, fraud, etc. and use fair and honest means for earning wealth. They should share their faultless earning with others who need their support (*K*, 44). The outcome of this virtuous living leads to the ultimate goal of life, namely eternal peace and bliss. What is achieved by renunciation in other paths is simply achieved by leading a faultless virtuous domestic life (*K*, 46). The householder's life involves greater responsibility, duties, and sacrifice than those of the other *āśrama*s. His virtuous family life itself is a greater penance, because it involves immense sacrifice and selfless service (*K*, 48). The family life is not a hurdle to spiritual enlightenment but an aid to evolution. A fruit should ripen naturally and become sweet. Family life provides a means for this natural growth, says Swami Satchidananda (Krishnaswami, 32). All the rough and tumble of domestic life and all the joys and sorrows naturally mellow a person. The duties and onerous responsibilities of married life blunt, curb and transform the animal tendencies, discipline the senses and curb passions and desires. When the angularities of the mind undergo corrections, the heart is purified. Then the divinity within manifests itself.

Thiruvalluvar describes the impermanence of wealth and compares it to the gathering and dispersal of a crowd at a show (*K*, 332). The wealth of a rich person is gathered gradually as people gather in a theatre, but it would disappear quickly just as the audience at the theatre melts immediately after the end of show (Krishnaswami, 68). Therefore, he advises, "Wealth is fleeting; hence when one gets it, it should be promptly spent on lasting works" (*K*, 333).

The above texts form a representative sample of how to live a virtuous life of a householder with a proper mindset about earning, maintaining, and spending of wealth. In spite of the loss of a major portion of Hindu literature, the existing Hindu literature is still so vast as to consist of fully 70 per cent of all the available literature in the world. The Hindu *dharma* is a way of life. Hence, there exists much literature with valuable suggestions on living with the sole objective of purifying the mind to attain perfection, the purpose of human birth.

Definition of Wealth

The wealth that the Hindu literature speaks of in beautiful poetic language has two elements: material wealth and relational wealth. Material wealth is tangible, physical, can be counted, and exchanged for goods and services. Everyone is familiar with this type of wealth and the necessity of it for living.

The relational wealth, on the other hand, is intangible, cannot be counted, cannot be exchanged in the marketplace for any material goods and services. But it is invaluable for satisfying the deepest inner urge, which cannot be satisfied by any material goods and services. It brings a sense of connection with oneself, with others, and with all. A lack of relational wealth produces alienation from self, from family, and from the community. The relational wealth of dutiful, selfless, non-attached actions, promotes individual growth by purifying the mind. Progressive mind purification allows a man to know the Self, akin to removing layers of dirt from a lamp in order to see it. Knowledge of the Self (*Ātman*) is liberation from the cycle of rebirths. Thus, the amassing of relational wealth is linked directly to spiritual growth. This individual growth must occur in harmony with other family members as well as all beings and the nature. The individual harmonious growth is the wealth of each member and the collective wealth of the family. *Thus, real wealth is the relational wealth.*

The above definition of wealth does not imply that the material wealth is to be spurned. In fact, material wealth is just as important as relational wealth. The individual body/mind complex is essential for each man's spiritual growth. This instrument must be maintained. It is akin to a car which must be kept in good condition to help transport a passenger to his destination. The needs of the body/mind complex must not be neglected (*BG*, 6:16). Material wealth is necessary to acquire food, shelter, and clothing. Specifically, in the case of the householder (*gṛhastha āśrama*), acquisition of material wealth (*artha*) is a requirement (*puruṣārtha*) and a duty. This duty is to facilitate the spiritual advancement of the people in the other three stages, viz. students, retired people, and renunciants, by offering (*yajña*) them the necessary food to maintain their body vehicles. The householder is expected to eat last after satisfying the hunger of the other three. Śrī Kṛṣṇa in the *Bhagavad-Gītā* has warned:

> The righteous who eat the remnants of *yajña* are freed from all sins, but the impious who cook food only for themselves (without sharing with others in charity) verily eat sin.
>
> — *BG*, 3:13

The householder's obligation is to assist in the harmonious spiritual growth of others before thinking of his own spiritual growth. The responsibility of the householder is all-encompassing and extends to all other beings as well as Nature (environment). The householder has an obligation to remember his ancestors (*pitṛ-yajña*), the hungry fellow men (*nṛ-yajña*), the animal kingdom (*bhūta-yajña*), the *devas* (*deva-yajña*), and the Absolute (*brahma-yajña*), in other words, the past, the present, the worlds of lower beings, and the world of higher beings (*BG*, 3:9). When the material wealth is thus deployed in selfless non-attached actions, it transmutes into relational wealth.

Hence, real wealth of any man is relational wealth of dutiful selfless non-attached actions. The material wealth is necessary for maintaining the body/mind complex and can be converted into relational wealth by right actions. *Fig*. 1 summarizes the interrelationship between material and relational wealth. Both are generated in a joint family. The material wealth may be used for forming (1). relational wealth by giving to charity,

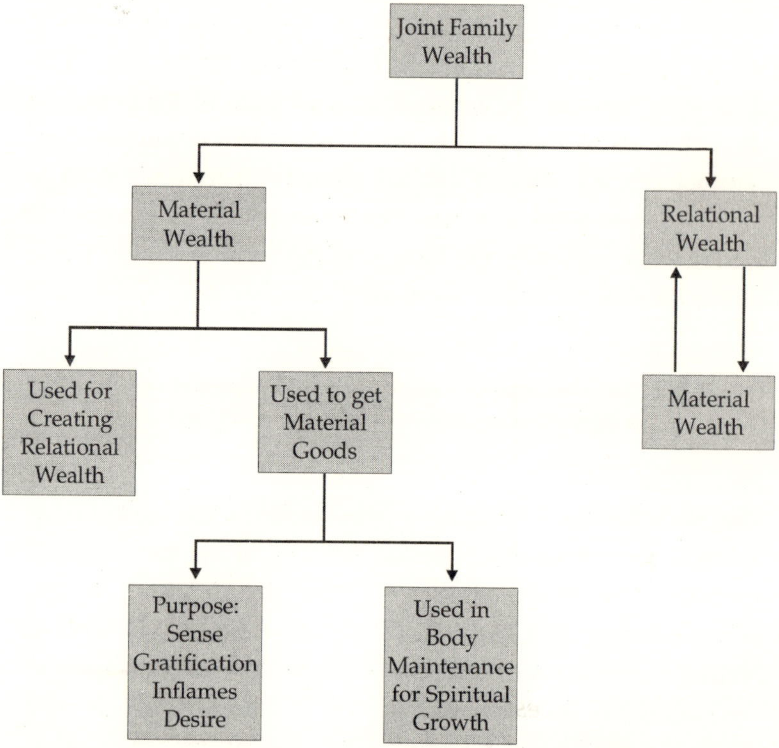

fig. 1: Wealth generation in a joint family

etc. or (2) buying material goods. The material goods used for body maintenance to assure spiritual growth of others as well as oneself, would qualify as relational wealth. Those goods that are bought to satisfy desires fail to add to relational wealth and result in inflaming and increasing desires.

Relational wealth generated in the joint family appears to create more material wealth which in turn again goes to generate relational wealth. From *fig.* 1, it becomes evident

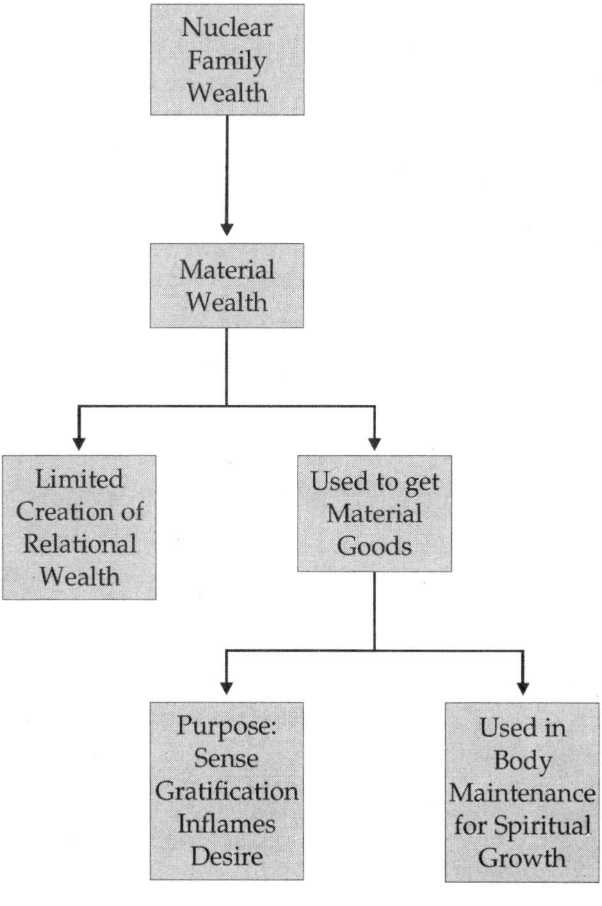

fig. 2: Wealth generation in a nuclear family

that a joint family tends to produce substantial relational wealth.

There is limited opportunity for relational wealth generation in a nuclear family wherein the main type of wealth earned is material wealth. This may be used to earn relational wealth by charitable contributions or to buy material goods. If material goods are used to gratify sense organs, then the desire for more goods is inflamed, causing overconsumption on the part of the individual. If the material goods are used to maintain body of others and oneself in a selfless unattached fashion, then relational wealth is being accumulated.

NUCLEAR VS. JOINT FAMILY RELATIONAL WEALTH

At first, the structure of the nuclear family may not appear to be a handicap for generating relational wealth. The material wealth generation requires a definite sense of separation from others. The mindset of "me" required for forming material wealth is diametrically opposed to the "us" required for developing relational wealth. In a nuclear family, the "me" includes the immediate nuclear family members, who are normally an extension of the ego of the individual, thus limiting the opportunity for developing relational wealth. This is generally the case, unless there is a strong disposition to care and serve others outside the family unit, arising from previous birth tendencies (*saṁskāra*). In a wealthy nuclear family, this disposition becomes less pronounced, as most of the day is spent in increasing, maintaining, and consuming the material wealth (Diwan, *Gandhian Economics*, 292). There is hardly any time to serve others. The ego rears its ugly head. The person may give to charities but it is usually to acquire name and fame in exchange. Śrī Kṛṣṇa describes such an individual in the *Bhagavad-Gītā*:

> Self-conceited, stubborn, filled with pride, and intoxication of wealth; they perform *yajña* only in name, for show, and not according to scriptural injunctions.
>
> — *BG*, 16:17

Nuclear family living fails to afford an opportunity for sharing material things foregoing certain pleasures, serving others, caring for ill relatives, and interacting with grandparents, the best teachers of values. As a result, the children lack the skills for developing relational wealth. On the other hand, the joint family living allows more discretionary time from task sharing, making it possible to engage in service activities. Availability of time is one of the critical factors in developing and sustaining a sense of connectedness, which no wealth can buy. Studies indicate that in a joint family, the shared household tasks distribute the work among members so that one person is not overburdened (Medora, Larson, and Dave, 415). Most importantly, as we are aware, it is not possible to quench the desire for material sense objects. As soon as one desire is satisfied, it brings many more in its wake, akin to putting fuel in the fire. Śrī Kṛṣṇa has advised the only method for attaining peace of mind in the *Bhagavad-Gītā*:

> One who abandons all desires and becomes free from longing and the feeling of "I" and "my" attains peace.
>
> — *BG*, 2:71

A certain amount of food, shelter, and clothing are essential for maintaining the physical body. However, after those needs have been met, an individual begins to, in the words of Diwan, fall prey to "overconsumption" (*Relational Wealth*, 327).

Diwan states that the desire for material wealth wanes with increase in relational wealth (*Gandhian Economics*, 285). The author of this paper observes an interesting phenomenon between the two types of wealth. When a person amasses relational wealth by adopting a selfless unattached approach to giving whether of wealth or service, material wealth tends to flow in naturally. When one gives, one starts receiving. The first reaction to this information is that it is being made up to encourage people to give more. However, it is more than encouragement. It is a basic truth. Thiruvalluvar maintains, "The life of one who hosts guests everyday will never face the calamity of poverty" (*K*, 83). This outlook of giving is observed in many entrepreneurs. N.R. Narayana Murthy of Infosys, a well-known successful entrepreneur of a technology firm in India, when asked what money means to him, replies,

> Beyond a certain level of comfort I think one's wealth should be seen as an opportunity to make a difference to society. The power of money is the power to give. Obviously it will have to be done in a gradual manner over the years, but there's no doubt that a majority of what we have will be given to public causes.
>
> — Dange and Govil, *Indian Entrepreneurs*, 21

Known for simple living, for travelling in economy class, adhering to strong ethics, Narayana Murthy is frugal and employs no servants at home. When it comes to his employees, he has built a world-class office complex for their use.

RESEARCH FINDINGS: JOINT FAMILY STRUCTURE FOSTERS RELATIONAL WEALTH

There is substantial research that joint family members have ample opportunity to earn relational wealth in two ways:

1. Joint families tend to have higher incomes and less expenses than nuclear families. Material wealth provides an opportunity to assist others, donate, and do other charitable works, thereby producing relational wealth. Thus, there is always a choice to

convert material wealth into relational wealth by dutiful, selfless, non-attached actions.

2. Living in a joint family itself affords constant opportunity to form relational wealth.

Research findings are as follows:

- Empirical evidence suggests that joint families tend to own more land and property.

  > Ownership of land is significantly associated with family type. Families with agricultural land tend to stay more in joint families. These results are in concurrence with earlier studies. — Gough, 1956; Nimkoff, 1959; Caldwell et al., 1988; S.A. Freed and R.S. Freed, 2000a, qtd. in Niranjan, Nair, and Roy, p. 634.

  In contrast, studies in India have shown that the "women heading single parent families are forced to take loans or get support from relatives (Chakrabarti, 1987; Satya Leela, 1991; Chen and Dreze, 1992) leading to stress and strain, and socioeconomic problems" (Premilla D'Cruz and Shalini Bharat, 2001, qtd. in Niranjan, Nair, and Roy, p. 634). With more wealth, joint families have an option to convert a portion of it into relational wealth.

- Joint families consume less natural resources being more efficient in usage. There is cost effectiveness experienced from living in one household, instead of two or more households. The cost of running a joint family is larger than a nuclear family, but significantly less than if all the nuclear families were to live separately. Members share their skills so less things have to be purchased. The younger children frequently wear the clothes of older siblings and cousins. It is an accepted practice to hand down almost all items including books, toys, clothes, bikes, baby furniture, etc. In very large families, it is economical to engage a tailor for making custom clothes, buying fabric in bulk, making for economies of scale. Efficient use of all household equipment, including cars, is made. Nothing sits unused. Wastage is minimized. Joint families are a perfect solution to preserve the biodiversity hotspots (areas rich in endemic species and threatened by human activities). Jianguo et al., in their article on "Effects of Household Dynamics on Resource Consumption and Biodiversity," state that:

> Reduction in average household size alone will add a projected 233 million additional households to hotspot countries during the period 2000-15. Rapid increase in household numbers, often manifested as urban sprawl, and resultant higher per capita resource consumption in smaller households pose serious challenges to biodiversity conservation.
>
> — p. 530

Living in a joint family reduces the burden on the environment and does not threaten the animal habitat. The conservation of resources and respect for nature is a form of relational wealth.

- There are numerous other ways that a joint family tends to reduce overall costs thus increasing income. It is customary for the family doctor to visit the house and see all those needing medical attention in one visit reducing medical costs. Baby sitting costs are eliminated as the need for such care is unnecessary. Textbooks which must be bought in India are shared reducing educational costs. An outside tutor can tutor several kids at the same time. The children learn most skills from each other easily. The children do not require formal instruction as they learn automatically by observing and interacting with a large number of other children and adults of varying ages. Entertainment costs are less. The cost-savings experienced provides an opportunity to accumulate material wealth providing a choice to transform into relational wealth.

- The joint family system forms a safety net for its members reducing the need for a costly national social security system. In a lecture given in 2001 by S. Gurumurthy, an economist from India, he stated that:

  > The biggest government expenditure in the Western countries is social security payments. In the USA, it is about 35 per cent to 40 per cent. In India, the family or the society bears the burden of social security, i.e. taking care of elderly citizens, unemployed brothers and sisters. With 65 per cent of households having a single earning member, Indian families contribute to the social capital through which the society sustains by itself.
  >
  > — Gurumurthy, par. 4

  In the United States, fully 40 per cent of the budget goes to meet the social security needs of the elderly, widows, minor children, and disabled, putting a heavy tax burden on the working population. The selfless caring for all members generates relational wealth.

- The joint family is largely responsible for the entrepreneurial activity, especially in the retailing sector, in India. India has 15 million retail businesses in contrast to the United States' 0.9 million retail businesses, the land offering the best free enterprise system in the world (*The Economist*, "Retailing in India,"

69). In proportion to the country's population of 1.1 billion, this amounts to four times more entrepreneurial activity in India, in retailing alone, compared to the United States. Such entrepreneurial activity exists despite many handicaps, including a licence *raj* in existence before the 1990s, prohibitively restrictive labour laws, impossibly outdated infrastructure, and onerous central, state, and local government rules and regulations. The small businesses are normally operated by combining human and financial resources of the joint family. This sharing and working closely together creates relational wealth. A small business tends to produce higher income for the owners, further affording an opportunity to convert into relational wealth.

- The NFHS survey indicates that there is a significant association between the level of education of the head of the family and family structure. As the education of the head of the family increases, he/she is more likely to live in a nuclear family as opposed to a broken nuclear family. Further increases in the level of education translate into more opportunities for work in industrially developed urban areas. As the cost of city living is higher, Niranjan, Nair, and Roy conclude that individuals are obliged to live with their relatives, causing an involuntary formation of joint family arrangement (634). This forced living structure creates an opportunity for formation of relational wealth. Higher education level is likely to indicate a better understanding of respective duties of each member, thereby increasing harmony among members.
- The author has conducted an informal survey based on a published CLSA report of Indian Entrepreneurs'

Hall of Fame, published in February 2006 issue. There appears to be a high correlation between joint family support and success in entrepreneurial undertaking (see Appendix 3). The relational wealth tends to generate material wealth, which in turn increases relational wealth.

- A sense of harmony is relational wealth. "For the Hindu family a sense of togetherness, family unity, and family harmony are of paramount importance" (Chekki, 1994, Misra, 1995, qtd. in Medora, Larson, and Dave 414). Medora, Larson, and Dave also concluded from their research that the joint family system provides a sense of closeness and harmony among members (415). Bhatti had earlier determined that Indian families are "characterized by extreme cohesiveness and a high degree of 'we' feeling. The members have mutual trust and interpersonal commitment. The atmosphere is saturated with regard and emotional warmth. The members of such families would not mind sacrificing anything for the welfare of one another" (Bhatti, 1986, 9, qtd. in Medora, Larson, and Dave, 415).
- Medora, Larson, and Dave have found empirical evidence that a joint family promotes "a feeling of support and overall well-being" (414). This is attributed to the fact that "the Indian culture has a strong built-in support system for family members of all ages, and all types of assistance is guaranteed in times of crises. The Indian family also works as a buffer and helps in managing stress and coping with it" (Misra, 1995, qtd. in Medora, Larson, and Dave 414). The family responds in bad times offering emotional, financial, and physical support including childcare. The benefits

to children raised in this environment are receipt of respect, a common emotional experience, and lifelong bonding with relatives (Sinha, 1988, cited in Medora, Larson, and Dave, 414).

- Research indicates that living in a joint family fosters a feeling of co-operation and dependability, thereby enhancing relational wealth (Medora, 414). This is due to an environment of love and concern among joint family members. Tolerance, adjusting to other members' needs, reliability, a common understanding among members, and the ability to sacrifice for the common welfare of all are some of the reasons given for happiness in a joint family (Verma, 1987, cited in Medora, Larson, and Dave, 414).
- Researchers report a fair and equitable division of family tasks in a joint family reducing overall burden on individual members. The parents in the nuclear family and specially single parent families have the burden of taking care of all household chores, grocery shopping, cooking, childcare, eldercare, running of numerous errands to keep the home running, and social entertainment and education of children during vacations (ibid., 415). This confirms earlier research in which the practical benefit of this living arrangement includes division of responsibilities among brothers, and housework among sisters-in-law, with others pitching in during times of illness, economic hardship they experience due to unemployment, or any of the numerous stressful situations encountered in daily life (Derne, 1994, cited in Medora, Larson, and Dave 415). For Western female entrepreneurs, a joint family would be a boon for running a successful business. They are faced with work/family conflict of immense

proportions. Louis Shelton, a researcher on female entrepreneurs on work/family conflict, identified three possibilities to alleviate the work/family conflict experienced by Western female entrepreneurs that included (1) role elimination; (2) role reduction; and (3) role-sharing (285). She fails to consider the resources available in a joint family system for women entrepreneurs. The success of Indian female entrepreneurs as well as working women can be attributed to the support available, a form of relational wealth, from the joint family members.

- Empirical evidence collected reports a lack of feeling of separation and an opportunity for readily available companionship within a joint family (Medora, Larson, and Dave, 415). This is a crucial form of relational wealth enjoyed by joint family members. This study tallies with a previous study that suggests that "individuals raised in cultures with collectivistic and familial values tended to be less lonely than those raised in an individualistic culture" (Sinha and Verma 1987, qtd. in Medora, Larson, and Dave, 415). Some of the elderly population in the Western countries experience significant amounts of loneliness with some wealthy individuals hiring paid companions to alleviate loneliness. In contrast, the older generation enjoys a greater respect and feeling of importance in the Indian culture, with the children and grandchildren seeking advice and deferring to them in general. The elderly are treated with care and love during times of illness with assistance coming not only from immediate joint family but also from distant relatives (Bhogle, 1991, cited in Medora, Larson, and Dave, 415).
- The joint family system provides an invaluable

opportunity for the young to learn from the old: the customs, the culture, the history of the country, as well as the personal family history. The value system can be transmitted clearly and impeccably, without the children attending a single class. The grandparents have the necessary time and patience to teach the young, difficult for even parents leading a placid life. It would be safe to state that the number of carefully nurtured and bright people found in India is due to a culture that loves and values the young, and takes great pains in educating them, akin to raising tender plants. Anil Agarwal, founder of Vedānta Resources, ranked number fourteen in wealth by *Indian Forbes 40*, attributes his success to his father and grandfather, insisting that, "They never let me slow down, including my grandfather who is 93 years old. Whenever I try to slow down a little, they say no" (Dange and Govil, *Indian Entrepreneurs*, 34).

- The tolerance found among Hindus is a major factor in successful joint family living and developing relational wealth. The Hindus (including Jains, Sikhs, and Buddhists)[1] are more likely to live in a joint family system than non-Hindus. Kolenda and Haddon have conducted a district-wise analysis of selected states in India that revealed that the high joint family districts had more Hindus and substantially fewer Christians than the low joint family districts (1987, cited in Niranjan, Nair, and Roy, 623). The Hindu families are driven by Hindu philosophy and values when living together. "Most Hindus do not separate religion/spirituality from day-to-day living. It is interwoven in the social and cultural milieu in everyday family life in the Indian community. Hinduism is a way of life" (Nandan & amp; Eames 1980, qtd. in Medora, Larson, and Dave, 417). Hindu joint families offer a sense of belonging and security which stems from the Hindu concept that, "All are really One." As the *Bṛhadāraṇyaka Upaniṣad* points logically, if there is no other, then what is there to fear (*Bṛ*, I.iv.2)?

The tolerance of Hindu *dharma* directly contributes to prosperity. Paul Johnson, an eminent British historian and author, in a *Forbes* article, correlates tolerance with prosperity around the globe, and conversely fundamentalism with poverty. He maintains that,

> It is the nature of the Hindu religion to be tolerant and, in its own curious way, permissive. . . . "When left to themselves, Indians (like the Chinese) always prosper as a community. There are now more millionaires in this group than in any other recent immigrant community in Britain. They are a striking example of how far hard work, strong family bonds and a devotion to education can carry a people who have been stripped of all their worldly assets." — "Want to Prosper?", par. 2

- The members share hospitality: different family members attend different functions keeping a presence in the community and someone is always home to greet guests and visitors.

CHALLENGES FACED BY JOINT FAMILIES

The above-mentioned strengths of living in a joint family is for an ideal family. Almost all families fail to operate at the ideal level. If the family is fortunate to have a head of household with the saintly selfless qualities, then the family functions relatively well. However, frequently there is politics and jockeying for power and money in the joint family, then the "me" mentality prevails instead of "us" mentality. When there is a tremendous discord among members, then it becomes advisable to separate rather than to continue living together. Frequently, the economic condition of some of the members prohibits separation causing strained relations and a general malaise in the family.

- Money is the most frequent source of discord among members. There arises a disparity when some members get more money in a family where the business is jointly owned. If there is inequity, the children as well as the adults sense it, and feel disadvantaged. Some members of the family hoard wealth secretly in case they need it for a rainy day, literally pilfering the family coffers. Dependent sisters-in-law, economically insecure, are frequently likely to engage in such practices eventually convincing their husbands to go along with them. Some would go so far as to buy land and property with titles in their names. In the old days, it was customary and considered good management, for the wife of the head of household to hide a portion of income for the welfare of all. The thought was, if it was not seen, it would not be spent. During financially strained times, this wealth was produced to avert bankruptcies in families. Jewellery has been a preferred form of investment that could be sold in bad times. In the Medora, Larson, and Dave survey, one of the things that the Indian youth would like to see changed is a lack of finances available to them (410).
- In the book, *The Family in India, Structure and Practice,* Shah explains the intricate details of the partition of property amongst the brothers, during the lifetime as well as after the death of the parents. This can be a time of trial, inequity, bitterness, and hostility. Even then, he goes on to say, the separated families still

continue to consider themselves members of a family, but the expectations and the intensity of family relationship decline (Patel, 214-27).

- "Co-operation and collectivism are integral to the Indian culture. Indians value co-operation and shared decision-making and undermine autonomy, initiative, and individualism" (Segal 1991, qtd. in Medora, Larson, and Dave, 414). From a Western point of view, where the individual is the centre and focus of the world, any threat to individualism and independence is conceived as being a negative attribute. The individual preferences carried to an extreme foster the "me" mentality detrimental to garnering relational wealth. The challenge in a joint family is to preserve shared decision-making for the benefit of all without stifling individual initiative and creativity. It is common to see in certain patriarchal families general enforcement of decisions from the eldest member or members. This affects the development of the decision-making skills of the younger members and sometimes produces a lack of confidence on their part to take decisive actions.
- While researchers acknowledge the positive role played by the joint family which thrives on care, commitment, concern, and sacrifice, these same factors foster interdependence and inhibition of self-identity (Sinha, 1994, cited in Medora, Larson, and Dave, 414). The lack of physical freedom bothers the younger generation. Specifically, the younger members object to restrictions with a desire to have more freedom and less parental control.
- In the Medora, Larson, and Dave survey, the students list lack of communication among the family members.

Deme considers emotional and physical affection an important part of communication (413). A reason for this perception could be that the Indians are embarrassed by public displays of affection and tend to avoid physical contact. Pais supplies another reason. It could be that the communication between parents and children tends to be one-sided with children expected to listen rather than participate in an active discussion (1997, cited in Medora, Larson, and Dave, 413).

- Madhu Kishwar, the editor of *Manushi,* India's leading magazine on social issues and human rights, has written extensively on dowry-related problems and calls it a British legacy in land mismanagement. The British, familiar with Victorian norms, gave land entitlements to "male heads of the family," bypassing India's then customary laws allowing various categories of secure entitlements to women. In this way, the titles of property became concentrated among men and paved the way for the disinheritance of women in general. Thus, the women became financially dependent on others and a liability. The dowry system has been used frequently as an equalizer. Another factor is that the sons have traditionally been responsible for the financial care of the elderly parents. In the absence of a national social security system to care for the elderly, the parents who have invested in their son's upbringing and education become insecure. She says that

> with the breakdown of the traditional joint family and the reluctance of many women to stay with in-laws, the insecurity of the groom's parents triggers an impulse to extract what they can from the bride's family at the time of their son's marriage.
>
> — *Protecting Women in Marriage,* 35

The joint families are certainly full of challenges. It is precisely these challenges that are instrumental in the growth of the individual members. The members have a choice to stay within this environment for mutual benefit or give up and form nuclear families. In certain circumstances, when the discord and bitterness rises to a level where all members become affected negatively, then it is more appropriate to separate to form nuclear families.

Conclusion

The ideal family structure for living during the householder stage of life is within the structure of a joint family arrangement. A joint family provides the members a greater opportunity than a nuclear family, to form material and relational wealth. Material wealth may be used negatively to quench the insatiable desires. Or it may be used to harness relational wealth. The amassing of this relational wealth results in progressive mind purification and spiritual growth of the individual. This growth is an aid to peace and tranquillity of mind and may culminate in self-realization. Thus, real wealth is relational wealth.

This article has been an evolving process and as such is twofold:

(a) It establishes the importance of joint family structure in amassing true wealth for the benefit and happiness of both individuals and communities.

(b) It makes clear that the findings are applicable to all families regardless of borders.

However, it is beyond the scope of this essay to discuss the possible ways to renew interest and acceptance of living in a joint family structure in the United States as well as the rest of the world. Many groups, including the government bodies, are able to facilitate this process. The various ways include but are not limited to the following actions that may be undertaken:

1. Educators may choose to teach alternate living style of joint family living, among others, from elementary school to college level.
2. The individual governing bodies may elect to pass favourable tax laws that encourage rather than inhibit living in joint families.
3. The media talk show hosts may adopt this important issue using various outlets available to them.
4. The different political parties may choose to place the issue of joint family on their agenda.
5. The sociologists at universities may wish to conduct further research on this subject.
6. The businesses may provide incentives to encourage formation of joint families by offering medical insurance to other members living in the joint family besides the immediate nuclear family.
7. The environmentalists could participate by educating the public on the benefits of living together for biodiversity conservation.

|| *auṁ tat sat* ||

Abbreviations

BG	*Śrīmad Bhagavad-Gītā*
Bṛ.	The *Bṛhadarāṇyaka Upaniṣad*
GDP	Gross Domestic Product
Is.	*The Īśa Upaniṣad*
K.	*Kural*

References

Dange, Aniruddha, Anshu Govil, "Indian Entrepreneurs' Hall of Fame", *CLSA: Asia-Pacific Markets,* February 2006.

Dange, Aniruddha, Vasudev Jagannath, Bharat Parajia, "Indians Adrift in China", *CLSA: Asia-Pacific Markets*, June 2004.

De, S. K. et al., eds., *The Cultural Heritage of India*, vol. 2, Kolkata: The Ramakrishna Mission Institute of Culture, 2003.

Diwan, Romesh, "Gandhian Economics: An Empirical Perspective", *World Futures* 56.3, January 2001: 279, *Expanded Academic ASAP*. Thomson Gale. Massachusetts Bay Community College, 16 June 2006. <http://find.galegroup.com/ips/infomark.do?>.

———, "Relational Wealth and the Quality of Life", *The Journal of Socio-Economics* 29.4, July 2000: 305, *Expanded Academic ASAP. InfoTrac,* Massachusetts Bay Community College, 16 June 2006.

Gurumurthy, S., Lecture, "Free Trade and Globalization Effects on India", Sunnyvale, CA, 10 May 2001.

Johnson, Paul, "Want to Prosper? Then Be Tolerant", *Forbes* 21 June 2004; 14 June 2006. <www.forbes.com/currentevents>.

Kauṭilya, *Arthaśāstra of Kauṭilya and the Cāṇakya Sūtra,* Varanasi: Chowkhamba Vidya Bhawan, 1991.

Kishwar, Madhu, "Protecting Women in Marriage", *Hinduism Today,* July/August/September 2006: 34-35.

Krishnaswami, O.R., *The Wisdom of Thirukkural*, Yogaville, Virginia, 2001.

Liu, Jianguo, Gretchen C. Daily, Paul R. Ehrlich, and Gary W. Luck, "Effects of Household Dynamics on Resource Consumption and Biodiversity", *Nature* 421.6922 (30 January 2003): 530(4). *InfoTrac OneFile*. Massachusetts Bay Community College, 14 June 2006. <http://find.galegroup.com/itx/infomark.do>.

Medora, Niluper P., Jeffry H. Larson, and Parul B. Dave, "East-Indian College Student's [*sic*] Perceptions of Family Strengths", *Journal of Comparative Family Studies* 31.4 (Autumn 2000): 407, *Expanded Academic ASAP*, Massachusetts Bay Community College, 16 June 2006. <http://find.galegroup.com/ips/infomark.do>.

Niranjan, S., Saritha Nair, and T.K. Roy, "A Socio-demographic Analysis of the Size and Structure of the Family in India", *Journal of Comparative Family Studies* 36.4 (Autumn 2005): 623(29).

Patel, Tulsi, ed., *The Family in India, Structure and Practice*, Thousand Oaks, California: Sage Publications, 2005.

Ranganathananda, Swami, *The Message of the Upanisads*, Mumbai, India: Bharatiya Vidya Bhavan, 2001.

———, "Retailing in India, Coming to Market", *The Economist*, 15 April 2006: 69.

Sankaracarya, Sri, *The Bṛhadāraṇyaka Upaniṣad*, tr. Swami Madhavananada, Kolkata: Advaita Ashrama, 1997.

Shelton, Louis M., "Female Entrepreneurs, Work-Family Conflict, and Venture Performance: New Insights into the Work-Family Interface", *Journal of Small Business Management* 44.2 (April 2006): 285(13). *InfoTrac*. Massachusetts Bay Community College, 14 June 2006. <http://find.galegroup.com/itx/infomark.do>.

Vivekananda, Swami, *The Complete Works of Swami Vivekananda*, vol. 4, Kolkata: Advaita Ashrama, 1984.

Appendix 1

Overview of Indian Economy

from <http://en.wikipedia.org/wiki/Economy_of_India>,
June 19, 2006

The **economy of India** is the fourth largest in the world as measured by purchasing power parity (PPP), with a gross domestic product (GDP) of US $3.63 trillion. When measured in US$ exchange-rate terms, it is the twelfth largest in the world, with a GDP of US $775 billion (2005). India was the second fastest growing major economy in the world, with a GDP growth rate of 8.1 per cent at the end of the first quarter of 2005-06. This recent economic growth has been a catalyst for India's growth as a great power and emerging superpower. However, India's huge population results in a relatively low per capita income of $3,100 at PPP.

The country's economy is diverse and encompasses agriculture, handicrafts, industries and a multitude of services. Services are the major source of economic growth in India today, though two-thirds of the Indian workforce earn their livelihood directly or indirectly through agriculture. In recent times, India has also capitalised on its large number of highly educated people who are fluent in the English language to become an important location for global companies outsourcing customer service and technical support call centres. It is also a major exporter of skilled workers in software services, financial services, and software engineering.

India adhered to a socialist-inspired approach for most of its independent history, with strict government control over private sector participation, foreign trade, and foreign direct investment. However, since the early 1990s, India has gradually opened up its markets through economic reforms by reducing government controls on foreign trade and investment. Privatisation of public-owned industries and opening up of certain sectors to private and foreign players has proceeded slowly amid political debate.

India faces a burgeoning population and lack of infrastructure, as well as growing inequality and unemployment. Poverty also remains a problem although it has declined significantly since independence due to the green revolution and economic reforms.

Gross Domestic Product (GDP)

Real GDP (at PPP) $3.633 trillion (4th) (2005)

Nominal GDP (at current exchange rates) $775 billion (12th) (2005)

Real GDP growth rate (at PPP) 7.1 per cent (32nd) (2005)

GDP growth rate 8.1 per cent (March-May, 2005)

GDP per capita $3,400 (155th)

GDP by sector agriculture (21.8 per cent),

industry (26.1 per cent),

services (52.2 per cent)

Demographics

Population below poverty line 25 per cent (2002 est.)

Labour force

482.2 million

Labour force by occupation (1999)

agriculture (57 per cent),

industry (17 per cent),

services (23 per cent) (2005-06)

Unemployment rate

7.32 per cent (1999-2000)

Production

Agricultural products: rice, wheat, oilseed, cotton, jute, tea, sugar scane, potatoes;

cattle: water buffalo, sheep, goats, poultry, fish

Main industries

Textiles, chemicals, food processing, steel, transport equipment, cement, mining, petroleum, machinery, software

External trade Imports

(2003) $89.33 billion f.o.b. (25th)

Major imported commodities: crude oil, machinery, gems, fertilizer, chemicals

Main import partners USA 7.0 per cent, Belgium 6.1 per cent, China 5.9 per cent, Singapore 4.8 per cent, UK 4.6 per cent, Australia 4.6 per cent, Germany 4.5 per cent (2004)

Exports $69.18 billion f.o.b. (35th)

Major exported commodities textile goods, gems and jewellery, engineering goods, chemicals, leather manufactures, IT, ITES

Main export partners (2003): USA 18.4 per cent, China 7.8 per cent, UAE 6.7 per cent, UK 4.8 per cent, Hong Kong 4.3 per cent, Germany 4.0 per cent.

Appendix 2

Family Types

from: Niranjan, S., Saritha Nair, and T.K. Roy.
"A Socio-demographic Analysis of the Size and Structure of the Family in India",
Journal of Comparative Family Studies
36.4 (Autumn 2005): 623(29).

Type of family*	**Definition**
• Single member	• The respondent who is alone
• Broken nuclear unmarried	• Head without spouse but with or without children
• Nuclear family	• This type of family includes Nuclear pair • Head and spouse with or without unmarried children
• Supplemented	• It includes three types of families:

* The family refers to all persons who are relatives of the head. It excludes domestic servants, boarders, and so forth. In urban areas of Maharashtra, Goa & New Delhi, unrelated members are more. The total unrelated members in the survey data in India are 2162 (0.4 per cent). (Chakravorty and Singh, 1991; Niranjan et al., cited in Niranjan, Nair, and Roy, 626).

nuclear	Head and spouse with or without unmarried children but with other relations who are not currently having spouses
	• Broken Extended Nuclear: Head without spouse but with other relations of whom only one has a spouse
• Supplemented: Broken Nuclear	• Head without spouse with or without unmarried children but with other unmarried/separated/divorced/widowed relation
• Joint family	• It includes both lineally extended and collaterally extended families
• Lineally extended: family	• Head and spouse with married son(s)/daughter(s) and their spouses and parents with or without other not currently married relation(s) (OR)
	• Head without spouse but with at least two married son(s)/daughter(s) and their spouses and/or
	• parents with or without other not currently married relations
• Collaterally: extended family	• Head and spouse with married brother(s)/sister(s) and their spouses with or without other relation(s) [including married relation(s)] (OR)
	• Head without spouse but with at least two married brothers/sisters and their spouses with or without other relations

Appendix 3

Joint Families & Entrepreneurial Activity

In an informal survey of fifteen entrepreneurs Hall of Fame,

Aniruddha Dange, Head of India Research of CLSA, interviewed fifteen successful entrepreneurs. They are:

- N.R. Narayana Murthy of Infosys
- Anand Mahindra of M&M
- Anil Agarwal of Vedanta Resources
- Dilip Sanghvi of Sun Pharma
- Ekta Kapoor of Balaji Telefilms
- Gautama Thapar of BILT and Crompton Greaves
- Jignesh Shah of Financial Technologies
- Kiran Mazumdar Shaw of Biocon
- Kishore Biyani of Pantaloon
- Raghav Bahl of TV 8
- Rajiv Bajaj of Bajaj Auto
- Rajiv Mody of Sasken Communications
- Sanjay Labroo of Asahi India Glass
- Sanjiv Bajaj of Bajaj Auto
- Tulsi Tanti of Suzlon Energy

The report is interesting as the personal interviews reveal some important information about the family structure and thinking of the entrepreneurs. Of the fifteen entrepreneurs, twelve operate in a joint family system. It is not clear from the interviews whether the remaining three entrepreneurs live or operate in a joint family system. The joint family does not mean that these entrepreneurs live in the same house with their parents and married brothers and their families, but the concept is extended somewhat. In wealthy families, it is common to own more than one house, but the business is jointly owned. Not only are such joint families connected economically, but socially the families interact on a frequent basis. Geographical closeness is also not a requirement for a family to be considered a joint family. The families due to business operations are spread out across India as well as the world to manage the various businesses and tend to travel frequently to meet. Thus, joint family is a state of mind of being together and of being connected regardless of distance. It is relatively easy to stay connected in this age of telephone, internet, and transportation. This is not conclusive evidence but it can be said that the support of the joint family system allows entrepreneurial activity to flourish. According to NFHS survey, only 42 per cent of the urban families are joint families. This proportion should also match somewhat for this group of entrepreneurs but here the joint family arrangement stands at 80 per cent.

The joint family not only provides moral support but provides financial support for entrepreneurial success. Jignesh Shah started his business with financial support from his family as well as by mortgaging his business. Tulsi Tanti who lives in a fourteen member joint family is placed eighth in the list of richest Indians in *Forbes* 40, with a net worth of $3.7b in year 2005. He started his business initially with loans from his family. He said that his wife supported his business completely without which no business would have been created. He even treats his employees as family members. Anil Agarwal attributes his success to his father and grandfather who did not let him slow down. It is suggested that the joint family system makes for business success.

10

Ageing and the Family System in India*

Jyotsna M. Kalavar and *D. Jamuna*

ACCORDING to the 2001 Census of India data, there were 71 million adults over the age of 60 years in India. Dual-career families, changing values, and nuclear family dynamics have created new concerns about the care of the elderly. Against the backdrop of such social change, India has seen a gradual rapid proliferation of "pay-and-stay homes" for the elderly. These homes cater largely to urban, middle-income seniors who can afford such an arrangement. However, on a continuum, these homes run the gamut from dormitory-style accommodation to upscale, resort-style arrangements. This project examined "pay-and-stay homes" in the four principal cities of south India, namely Chennai, Thiruvananthapuram, Hyderabad, and Bangalore. In this study, 150 residents of "pay-and-stay" homes were interviewed. This presentation will examine the senior resident's perspective on reasons for relocation to a "pay-and-stay" as well as elaborate on the various models of "pay-and-stay" homes. The extent of social contact and reported positive effect was greater than that

* This project was made possible by a Fulbright research grant awarded to the primary author from the Council for International Exchange of Scholars.

reported with sons. This appears to be a departure from traditional expectations placed on the male child for provision of late life care.

"The rising prosperity of India" has steadily become a topic of coverage by the media, including the boom in real estate, India's rising GDP projected to reach $1 trillion, the demand outstripping supply for luxury items, and the evolution of the call centre culture. Some authors have lamented the erosion of cultural values among the youth as concurrently evident with the rise in disposable income. Another slow, insidious change has also been occurring in India's social landscape — how elders are regarded and cared for.

Nearly half of the world's elderly population lives in the Asia-Pacific region (United Nations, 1993). The two most populous countries in the world, China and India, are expected to account for a major proportion of the world's elderly (Rajan, Sarma & Mishra, 2003). Like many of the world's nations, India's aged population is increasing both in absolute numbers as well as in proportion to the general population. The size of India's elderly population aged 60 and over is expected to increase from 71 million in 2001 to 179 million in 2031, and further to 301 million in 2051 (Rajan et al., 2003). By the year 2025, it is estimated that there will be nearly 165 million older adults (Population Reference Bureau, 1998). The 2001 Census showed south India leading with the highest number of elderly persons over age of 60 years, and it is projected to maintain this lead for the next 40 years (Rajan et al., 2003). Improved health, enhanced hygiene, and rapid medical breakthroughs are reasons cited to explain this "ageing" boom.

Parallel to demographic changes are other changes that have impacted the social landscape of India. A changing social landscape coupled with a demographic boom in the numbers of elderly have necessitated changes in urban living arrangements in India. Designated senior housing is a rapidly proliferating boom in urban India. Caring for older people, once considered a problem only in Western nations, poses an interesting challenge for India. While the majority of older adults in India live with their children or other relatives, approximately 30 per cent either have no family to live with or cannot live with the family they have (Ara, 1997). The "contraction" of the extended family is most apparent in urban environments. The decline of the joint family is an important factor that has undermined the position and status of the older adult (Ramamurti & Jamuna, 1991; Bose, 1994). At the same time, younger women, who traditionally have been providers of care for elderly family members, have entered the labour force in unprecedented numbers, thereby restricting the care available for the growing number of elders.

For many older adults, children (especially male children) represent an old age security. Modernization, technological advances, mobility, changing lifestyles and erosion of values have altered the face of India. The shortage of housing in cities, rising costs of living, and dual career families have led to changing priorities that affect the intra-family distribution of income in favour of the younger generation. The gulf between the generations is being further widened by the growing pressures of modern life — the crunch of time, space, and money (Bose, 1994). According to Dandekar (1996), "Even if unwanted, the old have to live with their children since most of them cannot afford to have independent households." Modernization, technological advances, mobility, changing lifestyles and values have altered the face of India. All these have impacted the individual security in late life that was previously accorded to older adults. Against the backdrop of a changing social landscape, many older adults of the middle-income category are choosing to live in an old age home.

Cultural Ethos

According to ancient Hindu scriptures, the lifespan of an individual is divided into four stages (*āśramas*), the first stage of *brahmacaryāśrama* (stage of a celibate student), the second stage of *gṛhasthāśrama* (stage of a householder), the third stage of *vānaprasthāśrama* (stage of gradual disengagement from worldly duties and social bonds), and the last stage of *saṁnyāsāśrama* (stage of complete disengagement leading to renunciation). The last two stages encourage "disengagement" but are hardly observed (Rao, 1993). Clearly, this system has undergone drastic change over the centuries since the original prescription.

In present-day situations, the values of *saṁnyāsāśrama* which include *vairāgya* (detachment) are generally practised within the family context. It is not uncommon for many elderly Indians to withdraw from society by going on long pilgrimages over extended periods of time akin to the wandering ascetic (Tilak, 1989).

There appears to be a parallel between this traditional Indian concept and the work of Cumming and Henry (1961) on disengagement notions (Vatuk, 1980). Their theory identified reduction of interaction with the environment among the elderly as being an eventual condition for the maintenance of life satisfaction. The existence of such a concept among Indians is of tremendous relevance in assessing late life experiences.

Old Age Homes

Old age homes (as they are known in India) have begun to expand rapidly in most metropolitan areas in India. According to Liebig (1999), less than 1 per cent of India's older population lives in old age homes. Ramamurti and Jamuna (1993b) reported that most of the old age homes are maintained by religious and voluntary organizations. The concept of old age homes is not new in India as there were such facilities to care for destitute older adults as far back as the eighteenth century (Nair, 1995). Noteworthy is the new breed of old age homes that are dubbed "pay-and-stay" homes. What is new in India is the concept of "pay-and-stay" homes that cater primarily to middle class older adults. Affordable only for middle or higher income families, they are being sought by many older adults as a viable alternative to a life of feeling marginalized and discriminated against. These older adults represent a cohort of individuals who had been socialized to venerate their elders. They are "pioneer residents" of "pay-and-stay" homes, being the first generation to live with strangers rather than family members.

This article will examine the experiences of residents of "pay-and-stay" homes in the cities of Thiruvananthapuram, Hyderabad, Chennai, and Bangalore.

METHOD

Sample Characteristics and Data Collection

The present study involved a total of 150 residents of "pay-and-stay" homes in the principal southern cities of Bangalore, Chennai, Hyderabad and Thiruvananthapuram. Using HelpAge India's current listing of "pay-and-stay" homes, the proportion of interviews in each city was determined. Since the maximum "pay-and-stay" homes were located in Bangalore than any of the other three cities, nearly 41 per cent of the respondents were selected from Bangalore. Similarly, Thiruvananthapuram had the least number of "pay-and-stay" homes among the four cities. Consequently, only 12 per cent of those interviewed were residents of "pay-and-stay" homes there. The types of "pay-and-stay" homes were categorized into the following groups: dormitory style accommodation, shared unit (3-4 persons per room), semi-private room (2 persons per room), private room, and deluxe suite. Of those interviewed, 12 per cent resided in the dormitory style accommodation and the most interviews were conducted with residents of semi-private rooms (27.3 per cent).

Majority of respondents were female (65 per cent). While the reported average age was 75 years (SD = 5), the age ranged from 65-90 years. Only 15 per cent of this sample reported living alone before relocating to an old age home. The rest reported living with spouse, children or siblings prior to relocation. More than half of the respondents (58 per cent) reported being currently widowed. Nearly a third of the respondents (30 per cent) reported having no children. Majority of the respondents reported being Hindu (83 per cent). This was followed by Muslims (7.4 per cent), Christians (6 per cent) and Others (Sikhs, Jains, and Buddhists) who accounted for less than 4 per cent of the sample. The educational profile was quite diverse for this population. While 5 per cent reported having less than 5 years of formal education, nearly 31 per cent reported 6-10 years of formal education. The average length of stay in the home was 4.3 years (SD = 2.1).

Respondents were interviewed by prior appointment in the facility in which they resided. Interviews were conducted privately (mostly in the forenoon), after an explanation was provided about the study and voluntary participation was solicited. Interviews were conducted in English often interspersed with the local language of the state. The interviews lasted for approximately 60-90 minutes.

Instruments

Participants responded to a detailed interview that included many open-ended questions about socio-demographic characteristics, social supports, perceptions of life in the home, self-reported health status, physical activity, evaluation of the home, etc. The Social Supports Inventory (Ramamurti & Jamuna, 1991) was part of the Interview Schedule along with The Self-Rated Health Index (Lawton and Brody, 1969).

Results

An examination of these homes suggests that the depiction of a typical "pay-and-stay" home profile is short-sighted. The management of these homes ranges from charitable/religious trusts that charge a basic minimum to those run by for-profit institutions. Besides a monthly fee, the initial accepted deposit may vary from a few thousand rupees to several lakhs of rupees. Such deposits may be partly refundable or may be completely non-refundable. The accommodation itself may range from dormitory style accommodation with little privacy to independent housing units that offer luxurious accommodation with complete privacy. Some of the middle to higher-end homes offer recreational/social/spiritual activities that involve the residents while others do not provide such opportunities.

The primary reason cited for relocation was analysed for the first open-ended question, "Why did you move to this home?" Childlessness, adjustment issues, and non-availability of daytime care by working children were the three most common reasons cited. Together, they accounted for nearly half (42 per cent) of all the reasons cited by residents. Other reasons that were cited included children residing overseas, fear of crime, financial strain, and the difficulty of maintaining a home in late life. Nearly 9 per cent of the sample indicated that they had "no alternative" while 8 per cent pointed out that they moved "after the death of spouse." Only 4 per cent of the sample indicated that they did so as they "liked their independence."

In response to the open-ended question, "Was this move planned, anticipated or unexpected?," the following responses were generated. Nearly half (49 per cent) of the seniors indicated that this was a move that they had "anticipated" for some time. This was a "planned move" by 27 per cent of the sample. Movement into this old age home was reported to be "unexpected" for 23 per cent of the respondents. Several of them indicated that after some heated family discussion, an adult child packed their belongings and dropped them off at the home. Three of the respondents reported how their son and daughter-in-law drove them out of the home that they owned for several years. Many said they had visited an old age home earlier or knew someone who was a resident. Some also said that their child had been threatening to send them here so they knew this was to be anticipated. In other words, they had been exposed to the idea of institutional living in late life.

The next question was about their involvement in decision-making regarding the relocation to an old age home. While 59 per cent of the total sample indicated that they made the final decision to move, nearly 14 per cent indicated that they did so jointly with children. While some cherished independence, many stated that they decided to leave before the situation got intolerable. In response to the question, "Where would you most like to live?," one-third of the sample reported a preference for living in a "pay-and-stay" home (33 per cent). The next choice was "at home with family" (22 per cent) followed by "at home independently" (19.5 per cent). Other stated choices were "at an *āśrama*" (15 per cent) and "live abroad with children" (4 per cent). In response to the open-ended question on what they liked about the "pay-and-stay" home, in ranked order, the following reasons were cited: no household worries, timely food being available, and being away from family problems. References were made to daily

11 - Jyotsna Kalavar (standing), Pennsylvania State University

11a - Jyotsna Kalavar, presenting her paper

meditations, *pūjā* (ritualistic worship), *yoga*, and *prāṇāyāma* (controlled breathing). These adults reported that each day as part of their daily routine they spent a certain amount of time to further their religious/spiritual pursuits. They expressed how satisfying this was to them, and that it gave them considerable peace and relaxation. Similarly, in response to what they disliked about the "pay-and-stay" homes, seniors indicated the "absence of family members," "monotonous schedule," and "nothing to dislike." Data on social networks indicated that kinship and non-kinship relationships featured prominently in descriptions of social networks. Besides family members, the caregiver at the old age home and friends were likely to be mentioned. On average, the reported network sizes were small. Though less in number, the visits made by respondents to family members were nearly comparable to the visits made by family members. It appears then that individuals in these old age homes maintain some form of social contact with family members. Residents were more likely to state that the contact came from a daughter than a son. And, they also indicated that they were most likely to visit their daughter's home than that of their son. This appears to be a departure from traditional Indian expectations placed on the male child for provision of late life care.

Discussion

In India, the demographic projections of ageing necessitate that the challenges of elder care must be suitably addressed now (Kalavar & Duvvuru, 2006). Unmistakably, urban India is witnessing a gradual move towards this living arrangement in late life. Many of the seniors had never conceived that they would be spending their autumn years outside of their home and away from their family. Some adults expressed that they were victims of psychological abuse within the family or they "left before the situation got intolerable." Tales of children taking over the family assets and driving the senior from their own home was not uncommon. Whatever happened to the *Taittirīya Upaniṣad* dictum of "Revere your mother as God. Revere your father as God?" The lust for wealth has overridden cherished values of elder care, and even led to elder abuse. Twelve centuries ago, the mystic poet, saint and philosopher Ādi Śaṅkara wrote in the famous composition, *Moha Mudgara* (popularly known as *Bhaja Govindam*):

> *As long as there is the ability to earn wealth, the family shows attachment. When this capacity is lost in old age, no one at home cares to even enquire.*

Not all seniors carried the burden of distress or reported being there under duress. Some seniors preferred this living arrangement over any other. These seniors pointed out that they enjoyed the freedom from the demands of running a household, they were answerable to nobody, they could engage in leisure pursuits when desired, and preferred to maintain "intimacy at a distance" with their offspring.

The extent of social contact and reported closeness with daughters was greater than that reported with sons. This appears to be a departure from traditional expectations placed on the male child for provision of late life care. Like many Western countries, it appears that in future the social obligations for elder care in India may lean towards daughters. Other researchers have cited similar observations (Jamuna, 1997; Anantharaman, 1979; Jamuna, 1991). In Jamuna's (1990) study, elderly respondents indicated a preference to live with daughters than sons. Reasons cited were strong emotional attachment and the high likelihood of receiving good care from them.

Living with strangers, some relationships had replaced or even transcended biological ones. Some of the care providers had become "offspring" to them while some of the administrators had assumed sibling roles. Singh (1999) reiterated the importance of staff and care-providers encouraging mobility and participation in daily activities of the home for the aged. And, the level of gratitude that the seniors expressed for what they had (a roof over their head, and timely meals offered) was astounding. Two themes stood out in their responses to the open-ended questions. First, that the situation could be worse so they were thankful for their present situation. Second, they accepted their present state as the fruit of *karma* so there was nothing to lament about. It has been pointed out by Chandra (1996) that Indians view deterioration in old age as inevitable, and suffering is largely seen as an outcome of past mistakes (Shah, Veedon, & Vasi, 1995). It remains unclear whether these older adults regarded their current situation in a manner that truly yielded no dissatisfaction or whether their reluctance to express dissatisfaction stemmed from cultural factors or fear of retribution from care-givers at the old age home. Several adults stressed the value of religiosity in late life. They pointed out the inner strength and contentment they derived from their participation in meditation, *yoga*, and religious worship. The role of *karma* was found to be an important psychological marker of successful ageing among Indian elderly (Ramamurti & Jamuna, 1992; 1995). It is not surprising then that many of these older adults indicated that they had no sources of dissatisfaction and were accepting of their situation.

From the number of homes that are proliferating, it is expected that such "pay-and-stay" facilities will gradually establish themselves as a viable late life arrangement, especially in urban India. While the numbers may be increasing as an outcome of high demand, there is clearly a paucity of data about seniors residing in these homes. In one study by

Bagga (1997), depression and listlessness were reportedly pronounced among residents in the home for the aged in Pune where they lived as guests and got cooked food with no hassles of running a household. These facilities must take care to provide options such as opportunities for religious expression/ spiritual growth, and pay attention to those factors that enhance the quality of life in late life. Options may include the establishment of spiritual activities, invited speakers, field trips, and intergenerational programmes with the broader community so meaningful relationships may develop.

Much of the gerontological literature in India has largely focused on the community-dwelling older adults (Ramamurti and Jamuna, 2000; 2006). Further research is recommended throughout India to develop a comprehensive understanding of the experiences of late life living in "pay-and-stay" homes.

References

Anantharaman, R.N. (1979), "Perception of Old Age by Two Generations", *Journal of Psychological Researches, 23,* 198-99.

Ara, S. (1997), "Housing Facilities for the Elderly in India", *Ageing International*, 23, 107, 114.

Bagga, A. (1997), "A Study of Women in Old-Age Homes of Pune", in Chakravarty, *Life in Twilight Years*, Kolkata: Kwality Book Company.

Bose, A. (1994), "Policies and Programmes for the Ageing in India", *The Ageing Asian Population*, 71-75, New York: United Nations Report.

Chandra, V. (1996), "Cross-cultural Perspectives: India", *International Psychogeriatrics*, 8 (3), 479-81.

Cumming, E. and W. Henry (1961), *Growing Old: A View in Depth of the Social and Psychological Processes in Aging*, New York: Basic Book.

Dandekar, K. (1996), "The Socio-demographic Profile of the Old", *The Elderly in India*, New Delhi: Sage Publications.

Jamuna, D. (1990), "Caring for Elderly Women: Perspectives of the Turn of the Century", *Journal of the Indian Academy of Applied Psychology*, 16(2), 17-22.

——— (1991), "Perception of the Problems of the Elderly in Three Generational Households", *Journal of Psychological Researches,* 35, 99-103.

——— (1997), "Public Perception on Caregiving — Then (1984) and Now (1994): An evaluation", in Chakravarti (ed.), *Life in Twilight Years,* Calcutta: Kwality Book Company, pp. 365-74.

Kalavar, J., J. Duvvuru (2006), "Senior Residents of 'Pay and Stay' Homes: An Examination of Health and Physical Activity", *Indian Journal of Gerontology,* vol. 20, nos. 1 & 2, pp. 21-34.

Lawton, M.P. and E.M. Brody (1969), "Assessment of Older People: Self-maintaining and Instrumental Activities of Daily Living", *The Gerontologist,* 9, 179-86.

Liebig, P. (1999), "Using Home Modifications to Promote Self-maintenance and Mutual Care: The Case of Old Age Homes in India", *Physical and Occupational Therapy in Geriatrics,* 16, 79-99.

Nair, T.K. (1995), *Care of the Elderly: Directory of Organizations Caring for the Elderly in India,* Chennai: Center for the Welfare of the Aged.

Population Reference Bureau (1998), *1998 World Population Data Sheet.* Washington, D.C.: Author.

Rajan, S.I., P.S. Sarma, and U.S. Mishra (2003), *Demography of Indian Ageing, 2001-2051: An Ageing India,* pp. 11-30, P.S.R. Liebig, S.I. New York: The Howarth Press, Inc.

Ramamurti, P.V. and D. Jamuna (1991), "Social Supports Inventory for the Elderly", *Journal of Psychological Researches,* 36(2), 133-36.

——— (1992), "Aged in Developing India: Aging and Society", *The Indian Journal of Gerontology,* 4, 1-6.

——— (1993a), "India", in E.B. Palmore (ed.), *Developments and Research on Aging: An International Handbook,* pp. 145-58, Westport, CT: Greenwood Press.

——— (1993b), "Some Predictors of Life Satisfaction in an Indian Sample", *Indian Journal of Gerontology,* 8(12), 18-23.

——— (1995), "Perspectives of Gero Psychology in India: A review", *Indian Psychological Abstracts,* 2(2), 207-67.

——— (2006), "Geropsychology in India: ICSSR V Survey", *Indian Journal of Social Science* (in press).

——— (2000), "Evaluation of Old Age Homes, Day Care Centers, Mobile Medicare of Andhra Pradesh", Report submitted to Ministry of Welfare, Government of India, New Delhi.

Rao, V.A. (1993), "Psychiatry of Old Age in India", *International Review of Psychiatry*, 5, 165-70.

Singh, D. (1999), "Day Centres and Home for the Aged", in A.P. Bali (ed.), *Understanding Greying People of India*, New Delhi, Inter-India Publications.

Shah, G., R. Veedon and S. Vasi, (1993), "Elder Abuse in India", *Journal of Elder Abuse & Neglect*, 6(3/4), 101-18.

Tilak, S. (1989), *Religion and Ageing in the Indian Tradition*, New York: SUNY Press.

United Nations (1993), *Demographic Indicators of Countries: Estimates and Projections*, Sales Publications, No. E 82, XIII.5.

Vatuk, S. (1980), "Withdrawal and Disengagement as a Cultural Response to Aging in India", in C. Ferry (ed.), *Aging in Culture and Society*, 126-48. New York: Praeger.

11

Scientific Values within Indian Family Practices

Bal Ram Singh

Many of the essential values of ancient Indian life embodied in Vedas, Purāṇas, and Epics are relevant to modern world although there is a dearth of understanding and practice of those values in modern contexts. Consequently, the traditional values espoused by sages and saints are being considered irrelevant today. A scientific analysis of these values may generate interest and understanding to promote their use for modern problems.

Traditional, cultural, and social practices in India almost universally involve families, relatives, and friends. The joint family system in India, and to a certain degree in other places, is more amenable for personal, societal, and planetary development. However, scientific values have always been prone to be misused through ignorance, bias, and selfishness, leading to social evils, and to the exploitation of society and environment. This article focuses on many of the ancient traditions still in practice at least in rural India at individual, societal, and environmental levels. There is sound scientific evidence to suggest that by living in a supportive family environment there is substantial personal growth, both physical and mental. Studies have shown that a joint family system is helpful to patients in health and health care of individuals' several diseases. Many of the practices at the societal level (such as marriage), although under substantial pressure in modern times, find scientific backing from neuroscience and genetics. Finally, numerous rituals and traditions in rural India (such as *yajña*, use of *neem* (*Azadirachta indica*), following joint family system, etc.) are more amenable to environmental sustainability than anything modern science has been able to develop. A common theme in the practice of these traditions is the integration of the ideas at the level of family practice.

Introduction

INDIA is the only country that has several traditions derived from ancient Sanātana Dharma continuing in their practices till today. However, many of these practices have come under severe strain in the modern society, which has been exposed to scientific knowledge and technology. Many of the rituals, be in the form of *yajña*, worshipping rivers, ponds, and water wells, or worshipping trees and stones, are scoffed at by today's educated class. Similarly, traditions such as taking off shoes while entering kitchen, showering before cooking food, eating vegetarian food, or practising *yoga* have been looked at through sceptical eyes.

Many of the scientific ideas such as existence of light spectrum, gravity, mathematics, chemistry concepts, Ayurvedic health system, creation and destruction of the universe, are not being explored in the world with the rigour they need due to the lack of proper understanding of *sūtra*s and *sūkta*s in ancient texts of India.

Fortunately, many of the practices have survived within family traditions inherited over generations. Here we examine some of those examples.

12 - Bal Ram Singh, University of Massachusetts Dartmouth

12a - Bal Ram Singh, presenting his paper

Family Rituals

Family rituals vary in different parts of India, and are followed differently from family to family. A few examples are being presented below:

1. **Yajña**: Most Hindu families perform *yajña* either as part of their fixed annual/monthly/weekly rituals or as part of family celebrations, such as birthday, wedding, etc. In the rural areas at least there are *yajña*s performed to fend off diseases. Herbal offerings during *yajña* have now been shown to be helpful to the environmental purification (Nautiyal et al., 2007; Saxena et al., 2007a; 2007b). It seems there are different types of *havan* material (*sāmagrī*) to perform at different occasions. This would mean that burning different types of woods and other materials, such as *ghee* (clarified butter) produces different kinds of chemicals which may have differential effects on microbial growth.

While studies have shown reduction in microbial population in air and water in the vicinity where *yajña/havan* has been performed, it is important to note that a blind following of the ritual these days inside the house when such rituals are performed in cities may have adverse effects due to increased concentration of the chemical released. The scientific basis of this practice has been lost over a long period of time in the absence of robust discussion and understanding. With increasing use of artificial pesticides and their adverse effects on human health, it is increasingly being realised that natural pesticides may have to play an important role in managing pests and environment.

2. **Neem Tree:** In many parts of India, it is common for men and women, especially senior members of the family, to pour water on a *neem* tree, even before they take anything in the

morning. It is important to note that practices like watering *neem* tree continue in India only through family traditions.

While growing up in rural India I could never make sense of this when my mother religiously poured a *loṭā* (vessel) full of water on a *neem* tree soon after taking her bath. Her logic was that there is Śītalā Mātā on that tree for whom she must offer water every day. She believed that if she did not offer the water every day, Śītalā Mātā will get upset, and diseases like cholera or chickenpox will fall upon family members. If someone was down with chickenpox, *neem* twigs will be placed in the room of the patient, as that was supposed to keep Śītalā Mātā happy. Before going into the scientific aspect of this practice, it is important to ponder over the wisdom and strategic thinking of those who had the knowledge and wanted to implement it in the society by integrating it with family practices. By making the practice important for family health, and placing the responsibility generally on the female head of the family, the idea was to ensure that there will be at least one *neem* tree near the house (usually in front of the house) so she can easily perform this ritual conveniently. Presence of a *neem* tree in front of the house has many other uses, including using the twigs for brushing teeth for people who either do not want to use modern toothpastes or may not be able to afford them.

The narrative of Śītalā Mātā in the villages is that if the goddess who resides in the *neem* tree is not provided water (and flower, which also guarantees other plants around) before the head woman of the family partakes any food or drink, the wrath of the Śītalā Mātā will fall upon the family. This will make young kids of the family sick with cholera and pox. In older times, the only remedy was to have *yajña* in the house performed by a priest with *havan* and *mantra*s to pacify the goddess. Most of the time these things happen in the summer or during the rainy season in India.

A personal story intimately related to this narrative may help elaborate. At the age of about 10, I had developed chickenpox. There appeared to be an epidemic as many young children had developed chickenpox, and several of them even had died. My infection followed up with dysentery, which made me severely weak within a couple of weeks due to blood loss. Usual rituals of *yajña* and *havan* were performed more than once, but to no avail. My mother was constantly cleaning and comforting me, sitting on the floor next to my cot bed in front of the house (women of my family those days and to a certain extent even today would not sit on the bed, while men from the family or village are around). There was no question of summoning a doctor as that would anger the goddess. A day had come when my cries from stomach pain had become frail. Close and extended family members had stayed close by fearing my end. My mother had become stone-faced fearing the worst. My uncle, a bold and progressive man of his time, who was also the head of the family on the male side (my father had passed away a couple of months before I was born), decided to call a doctor anyway. According to his recollection he felt that since I was probably going to die anyway, he wanted to try doctor's treatment as well, as nothing worse could happen with the goddess's fury. Of course, with that decision I am here to narrate the story.

This event had so much influence on me while growing up that I used to dismiss much of the rituals and practices (religious or otherwise) in the villages. As I joined high school to study science I became more arrogant against many of the family practices, including my mother's daily routine of offering water to Śītalā Mātā on the *neem* tree. I used to make fun of what my mother said or believed about such things. However, she had a very different take on it. She had resolved more strongly to carry on with her practice, in addition to her *mannat* (wish) that she was to take me to Vindhyachal Bhagavatī (goddess of Vindhyachal), as she believed that I was cured more because of her *mannat* and *vrata* (vows) for goddesses, Śītalā and Vindhyachal Bhagavatī. I obviously did not believe in any of those things, although I did not question them specifically out of respect for my mother's belief and comfort that I was going to be fine as long as she had those goddesses on my side with her practices and *vrata*s. I did oblige her in 2001 by accompanying her to Vindhyachal for fulfilling her *mannat* to the goddess. I did it more for my mother's peace of mind than necessarily accepting her premise that I was saved due to her *mannat* rather than the treatment of the doctor.

However, these events did leave an impression on me, and I have started rethinking my views, particularly since my research has involved infectious diseases for over 20 years — now with more and more questions on the use of pesticides, drug resistance in bacteria, and the need of sustainable practices in view of global warming. Moreover, a lot more information is now available on the chemistry involved in the valuable effects of *neem*, which is now considered as a major source of natural antiseptic and pesticide (Schmahl et al., 2010), and is included in many herbal products and Ayurvedic medicines (Subapriya and Ragini, 2005).

Suddenly, the events which led me to despise many of the traditional practices are bringing back ideas to reconsider the values of those practices. First of all a description of the Śītalā Mātā from Wikipedia points to the following:

> Shitala is accompanied by Jvarasura, the fever demon, Olai Chandi/Olai Bibi, the goddess of cholera, the Chaushatti

> Rogas, the sixty-four epidemics, Ghentukarna, the god of skin diseases, and Raktavati, the goddess of blood infections. Shitala is represented as a young maiden crowned with a winnowing-fan, riding an ass, holding a short broom (either to spread or dust off germs) and a pot full of pulses (the viruses) or cold water (a healing tool). Among low-caste Hindus and tribal communities, she is aniconically represented with slab-stones or carved heads. Sometimes, she is said to be carrying a bunch of *neem* (*Azadirachta indica*) leaves, an ancient Ayurvedic medicinal herb that is very much an effective remedy to most skin diseases even today.

It now makes sense to see how a scientific knowledge was made part of the society in practice that was passed on from generation to generation. The fact that watering a *neem* tree in the name of a goddess with traits to provide medical relief or spread disease was made a traditional requirement before partaking any food or drink, linked it to the life's essential requirements. Linking the presence of Śītalā Mātā with tree, and her influence on the health of the family adds to the responsibility of the elders in the family to ensure the satisfaction of the goddess with the care of the tree. This made sure a *neem* tree at home and its nurturing. Many of its antiseptic effects are expected to be automatically available just by fragrance, seeds, and leaves. *Neem* extracts are used to manufacture from toothpaste, soap, to many Ayurvedic medicines. Twigs and leaves are still used in the rooms where patients of infectious diseases are housed. Such practices are retained within the family as responsibilities are transferred upon either passing away of the responsible person or when that person becomes unable to perform such family duties.

Modern science is struggling with making scientific living a part of the society. As an example, people in the United

States hardly follow the food pyramid recommendations of the United States Department of Agriculture (USDA) for their nutritional requirements. There is much to be learned from ancient Indian knowledge to live healthy, and more importantly to integrate the knowledge within the family practice to continue the tradition generation after generation.

Other Family Rituals and Practices

There are several other family rituals and practices which continue to survive in the rural India, and were at some time adopted for scientific reasons. These include no trespassing of the kitchen with shoes on, requirement of fresh bath and putting on clean clothes for the person cooking the food, eating freshly cooked food, including large portion of vegetarian food even for those who include meat and fish in their diets, performance of 16 major *saṁskāra*s (from conception to death) with special rituals (each having deep scientific and philosophical meanings; e.g. beating metal plates at birth for making people aware of a newborn to cremating the dead which is the most environment friendly way of disposing the dead body), and applying cow dung paste on the floors to disinfect, among others. Each of these rituals and practices is based on scientific reasoning and values.

Marriage and Family Life

Marriage is the beginning of family life; as written in other chapters, it forms the basis of life and society. Marriage in India has many aspects — spiritual, philosophical, social, economic, and legal amongst them. Some of these aspects are elaborated in the chapters by Divya Tripathi and Madhusudan Jhaveri. Scientific practices are visible in almost all these aspects.

Indian marriage traditions are generally based on *jāti* (caste) and *gotra* (family lineage). In most cases marriage within the same *gotra* is not recommended. In some communities, these recommendations are very strictly followed. For example, north Indian Khāp group is trying to enforce the social "ban" on the marriage within the same *gotra* (Divya, 2009). In most of India, marriage is generally performed within one's own *jāti*. While inter-caste marriages are happening in cities — although not common — *jāti*-based marriage remains the norm in rural India.

While social scientists and liberal society abhor marriage restrictions based on *jāti* and *gotra*, these practices are not without scientific merit, particularly marriage within *gotra* which may result in marriages within distant family members. While it is generally difficult to estimate the accurate risk, since history of *gotra* is not accurately known, nevertheless, based on observations with cousin marriages common in some sections of Pakistani society in Britain, it is clear that endogamy with respect to *gotra* will increase the chances of diseases from double recessive genes (LeFort, 2010). While the risk of birth defects is less than 3 per cent over normal, infant mortality among cousin progenies can run over 10 per cent, and pre-reproductive deaths among first double cousin progenies could be over 40 per cent. Translating these findings to *gotra* marriage risk needs more research. However, considering Indian traditions to be conservative it is understandable why *gotra*s may have been designed in the first place, and how same *gotra* marriage may not be a good idea even if the risks are not as much as in marriage between first cousins. In any case, there is no society anywhere in the world where such social behaviour has been practised for so long through family traditions.

Another aspect of Indian marriage has been generally the marriage being performed within the *jāti*. This would be an example of endogamy with respect to the *jāti* or caste. In addition to social and likely family's professional compatibility, it seems there may be some evolutionary traits involved in marrying girls not far away from the genetic pool of their fathers. In a couple of studies young college women were provided a box containing shirts worn by men for a couple of days, and requested to rate the smell of the boxes for pleasantness. It so happened that women rated the smell of shirt from men who were distantly related to their fathers, but not mothers (Furlow, 2008). Further analysis of the genes of these men and women found that human leucocyte antigen (HLA) genes (also known as major histocompatibility complex or MHC genes) determine the body odours (Jacob et al., 2002; McClintock et al., 2005). In addition to providing basis for odour preference the MHC genes are also responsible for immunoreaction, and may have conservative evolutionary utility for the offspring. It was found that women did not prefer odour of men who had less than one common allele from her inherited alleles. The data showed maximum preference for an average of 1.4 inherited alleles (*fig*. 1). Other studies have shown that women do not prefer odours of men with too many or too little common MHC alleles (cf. Jacob et al., 2002).

These findings of odour preference and common inherited MHC alleles coincidentally agree with the practice of endogamy practised by marrying within a *jāti* yet not preferring marriage within a *gotra*, as is practised in India, particularly among most Hindu, Buddhist, Sikh, and Jain populations. In south India, however, there is a practice of cousin or maternal uncle marriage practice. In large majority of the cases, though, the practice appears to mirror scientific observation, at least qualitatively. More research on such topic, particularly in India will likely provide relevant information.

In summary, both genetic disorder studies and odour preference/common MHC allele studies indicate that Indian family practices are consistent with scientific observations. While there is no evidence to suggest these practices were prescribed with scientific knowledge we currently possess, it would be extraordinarily helpful if a rational basis of such practices were discovered.

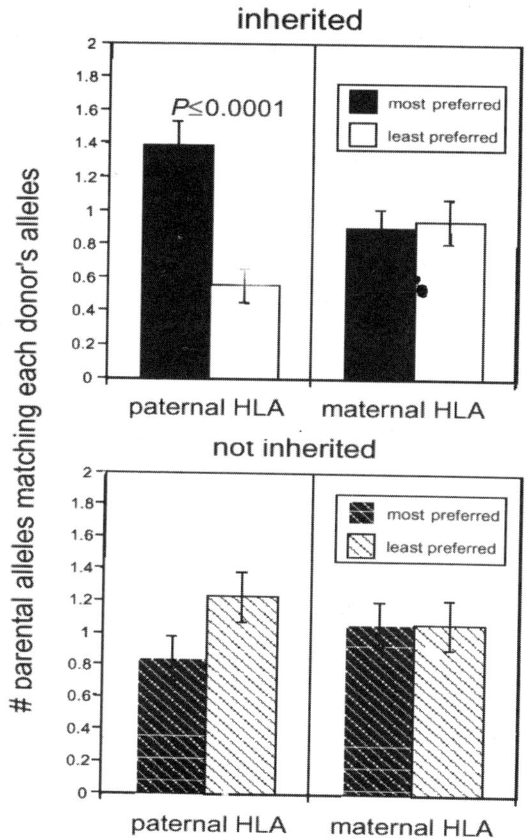

fig. 1: Effects of inheritance and parental origin of HLA alleles on odour choice. Number of allele matches between the paternally and maternally inherited alleles of each woman (*n*=49) and the alleles of her most preferred odour donor, compared with the number of matches with her least preferred donor (taken from Jacob et al., 2002).

Environmental Preservation and the Joint Family System

Accepting dhārmic values allows one to be free of bias, and thus creates a more just system which can build a progressive and developed society. One of the systems that has remained a pillar of Indian society is its joint family system. A joint family system is not sustainable unless dhārmic values are employed where selflessness becomes the operating principle. Scientific research has shown that joint family system is critical for environmental protection.

According to a report (Lazarof, 2003), the researchers have found that across the world, in both developed and developing countries, households are getting smaller, and there are many more of them. Multigenerational living arrangements are giving way to couples or individuals moving out on their own. In addition, rising divorce rates mean families that used to live in one dwelling now occupy two, and ageing populations mean more parents living in households separate from their grown children. The result is often urban sprawl and less efficient housing for the same number of people. For example, a refrigerator uses about the same amount of energy whether it belongs to a family of four or a family of two. Each household takes up space, requires resources to construct, and fuel to heat and cool it. Increased energy consumption also increases the emission of greenhouse gases, which is believed to contribute to global warming. The study was carried out by the scientists from Michigan State University (MSU) and Stanford University. Professor Jiaguo "Jack" Liu of MSU said, "Freedom and privacy come at a huge environmental cost."

The research findings suggest that in 76 countries containing biodiversity hotspots, between 1985 and 2000 the number of households grew by 3.1 per cent a year, whereas the population increased only 1.8 per cent. Meanwhile, the number of people living in a single dwelling dropped from 4.7 to 4.0. It was estimated by scientists that had average household size remained the same in hotspot countries during the 15-year period, there would have been 155 million fewer households overall, meaning less pressure on biodiversity. Hotspot countries studied included Australia, India, Kenya, Brazil, China, Italy and the United States.

"Ignoring population growth, reduction in household size alone is projected to add 233 million households to hotspot countries between 2000 and 2015," said Stanford ecologist Gretchen Daily. In the 65 non-hotspot countries, similar trends were found, although the magnitudes of change were less. In 1985, the average household size was 4.7 in hotspot countries and 3.7 in non-hotspot countries. By 2015, the average household size in hotspot countries is expected to be 3.4 persons, and in non-hotspot countries, it is expected to be 3.6 persons.

According to reports Liu has contended that the increase in household numbers even in non-hotspot countries directly influences important biodiversity on a national and local scale. Indirectly, global environment will be affected in such patterns as more energy consumption and release of more greenhouse gases. Even in regions where population size decreased, such as in New Zealand, the number of households increased because of a reduction in household size.

The "double toll" a reduction in average household size takes on the environment, the scientists believe, includes more land use and more materials consumed for construction, and a lower efficiency of resource use per person. In hotspot countries, where this trend is most prevalent, the authors believe there may be severe limits on efforts to conserve species, thus "degrading the ecosystem services that biodiversity delivers to humanity."

Joint Family and Health

Joint family also has health implications for individuals, particularly the elderly. It is estimated that there were about 75.9 million elderly people in India in 2001; one out of every 12 persons was aged 60 years or more in 2001. According to Chanana and Talwar (1987), this phenomenon, coupled with rapid social changes resulting in the gradual breakdown of the traditional joint family system and ever-increasing financial constraints at the national level, is likely to pose serious problems for the elderly.

According to another report (Krishnakumar, 2003) a major problem in the management of dementia patients in India now, according to Vijay Chandra, is the disintegration of the joint family system and the emergence of nuclear families, which has affected the care of the aged the most.

"We are getting caught in a no-win situation. There is no institution in place to take care of the elderly, nor is the traditional joint family system that takes care of the elderly intact," stated Chandra. "Patients with dementia, particularly the elderly, are best taken care of at home and not in an institution," he added.

A more recent study has shown that loneliness is hazardous to health. There seems to be a genetic basis for the loneliness which determines the reaction of different people differently to the same situation of social isolation. Moreover, people are prone to feel loneliness even if they have people around them. Functional magnetic resonance imaging to measure metabolic activity in the brains of 23 undergraduate women at the University of Chicago showed that lonelier individuals exhibited less activation in the ventral striatum (*fig.* 2), a component of the brain's reward circuitry, when they viewed pictures of smiling faces (Miller, 2011). Loneliness may also affect the prefrontal cortex, a region important for what cognitive scientists call executive control.

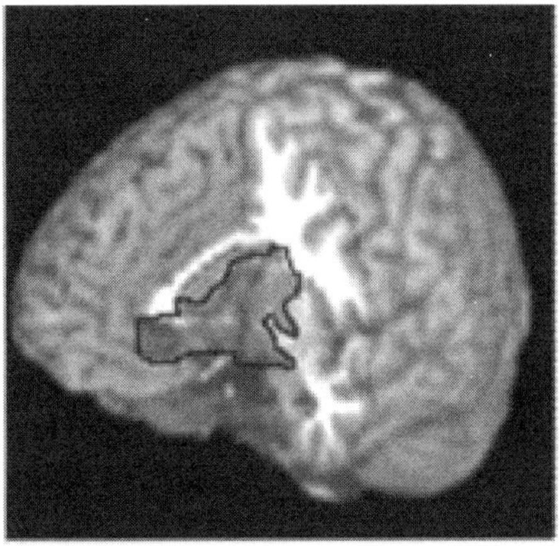

fig. 2 : Lonely people take less enjoyment from social interactions and exhibit less activity (area marked by the black line) in the ventral striatum (taken from Miller, 2011).

In experiments with human subjects it was found that lonely people exhibited increased activity for several genes encoding signalling molecules that promote inflammation and decreased activity for genes that normally put the brakes on inflammation (Miller, 2011). They also showed diminished activity in genes that help mount a defence against viral invaders.

It has been suggested that social isolation increases the risk of death about as much as smoking cigarettes and more than either physical inactivity or obesity. It is important to understand the state of loneliness. It seems to be the subjective experience of loneliness that is important for people's well-being rather than any objective measure of social connectivity (the number of close contacts someone has, for example). This suggests that people need to feel relevantly connected to others whose company they keep. It is therefore important that people continue to play a role in the company of others around. This is important specially for older people, who in many Western societies live away from home in senior citizen homes, a trend that is starting in India as well (see the chapter by Jyotsna Kalavar). In such a situation, while they may have company of people they may still feel socially lonely. Keeping elders at home means they remain connected to the family (with young children for whom they become a resource) and friends.

A joint family where uncles, aunts, brothers and their families live with grandparents provides the most amenable situation for everyone to remain involved with each other in a meaningful way while avoiding loneliness for everyone. These days even young men and women feel lonely, which increases their stress level leading to health risks.

Problems with the Joint Family Practices

Joint family system is continuously shrinking even in India. The reasons are many, primarily due to industrial progress and movement of a large population to cities. Furthermore, India has lost its cultural mooring since independence, as the Westernized education has effortlessly placed many of the traditional values under the rug. There has not been any effort to study, analyze, and promote useful values of traditional India.

Roots of such a situation are perhaps deeper in the history, and rest in the limited knowledge and misunderstandings of the dhārmic basis of the Indian culture. One of the major reasons has been the foreign rulers of India for the past 1,000 years or so. However, one has to only wonder why the institutions which have survived these foreign rules have not been able to bring out the true understanding of ancient wisdom to the general public. Part of the reason is, of course, the nature of these institutions which have been kept outside the mainstream educational process, but the other part of the problem is the distant past of the knowledge which has survived only as a record or assorted practice at individual and family levels, and not as an organized practice which generally evolves with the society.

Indian dhārmic traditions exhort everyone to be objective, detached, and practise equanimity in life, let alone in the examination of subjects for study and understanding. Indian traditions therefore are more robust to the scientific approach than other traditions. The term *dharma* implicitly incorporates the objectivity, and requires selflessness for its practice. Such a practice is absolutely needed to live and thrive in a joint family system.

Understanding the Dharma in the family

There are many definitions of *dharma*. Quite often it gets translated as religion, which is quite contrary to the original as well as even pragmatic meaning of the word *dharma*. According to Sage Kaṇāda, who provided the idea of the atom around 700 BCE, *dharma* is that which governs the birth or begins to rise and ultimate accomplishment (death) of everything.

yato 'bhyudayaniḥśreyasasiddhiḥ sa dharmaḥ | — *Vaiśeṣika*, 1.2

This is not just a secular definition of *dharma* but a scientific one. It refers to all those forces involved in governing appearance and disappearance of material and non-material things in this universe. When the meaning of *dharma* is appropriately understood, one has no choice but to turn to the nature to experiment and acquire the true meaning of *dharma*. This is a legacy of India or Hindus that must not be forgotten by those who call themselves Hindus and those who want to know more about Hindus, because the fundamentals of Hindu thoughts and traditions derive from such an understanding of *dharma*.

The understanding and practice of *dharma* is a subscriptive as opposed to a prescriptive system, and it applies to every aspect of life and living. So, there is a *dharma* of a son, a daughter, a father, a mother, etc., as much as the *dharma* of a tree, air, water, etc. People are generally free to subscribe to their own *dharma*, as they understand it from the experience of their family, community, natural environment, and of course, education. At the highest level, India does not have a record of injunctions for or against a given type of behaviour or practice. With a long experiment and experience for a society like India that has retained its continuing civilization for at least 10,000 years, many of its collective experiences have become traditions (translation of a Sanskrit word, *paramparā*, which refers to great knowledge). With passage of time, the basic meanings of many of the traditions get misunderstood or the traditions themselves become limited to rituals, which has caused much of social stagnation and at times problems for the society. Nevertheless India's fundamental principles moored in *dharma* remain eternal, the basic foundations of its traditions strong, and essence of its practices fairly universal.

The concept of *dharma* needs to be promoted in every religious tradition, because it carries elements of truth which can improve every culture and society in the world. It accepts and celebrates diversity, because of its reference point being the nature where diversity is rampant and is the basis of existence. Joint family provides the same diversity, and thus those who can practise their *dharma* appropriately can live in a joint family.

Concluding Remarks

Traditional practices in India have revolved around family values for their expansion and survival. While it is not clearly known to the modern mind how many of the traditional practices came into existence, these are consistent with modern scientific ideas. India's dhārmic traditions have not seen progressive evolution for several centuries, and current array of education system and scholarship is too confused to re-launch examination and adoption of Vedic knowledge to solve world's detrimental modern social, political, scientific, religious, climatic, and environmental problems.

Current global crisis related to environmental sustainability, socio-political issues, and economic system, combined with global communication is providing a fresh look at many of the Indic practices. It is, however, a challenging task to impart these ideas without demonstrating the utility of those practices at the individual and society levels. Family units will become the key to showcase these values. In the absence of teaching of these values in mainstream educational institutions, it is becoming difficult to understand the deeper meanings of the dhārmic philosophy. Alternative avenues need to be employed to grasp the essence of the tradition.

Vedic and Purāṇic traditions have used examples in epics and other stories to illustrate true meanings and intention of the traditions, but with the advent of philosophy of academic history which relies on limited documents rather than practice, there has been continuous deterioration of understanding of Vedic values. It is important to use the examples from *Rāmāyaṇa* and *Mahābhārata* to elaborate these problems, and to illustrate some of the true meanings.

It is hoped that the future generations will embark on revising the scientific tenor in society by using the examples of family traditions as database for ideas.

References

Chanana, H.B. and P.P. Talwar (1987), "Aging in India: Its Socioeconomic and Health Implications", *Asia-Pacific Population Journal*, vol. 2, 23-38.

Connor, S. (2008), "There's Nothing Wrong with Cousins Getting Married, Scientists Say", *The Independent*, 24 December 2008.

Divya, A. (2009), "Khap Wrath: Lovers and Their Kin Risk Boycott", *The Times of India*, 8 September 2009.

Furlow, F.B. (2008), "The Smell of Love: Why do Some People Smell Better to You? A Look at How Human Body Odor Influences Sexual Attraction", *Psychology Today*, 11 February 2008 (Article ID: 1174).

Greg, Miller (2011), "Why Loneliness is Hazardous to Your Health", *Science*, 331, 138-40.

Jacob, S., M.K. McClintock, B. Zelano, C. Ober (2002), "Paternally Inherited HLA Alleles are Associated with Women's Choice of Male Odor", *Nat Genet*, 2002 Feb; 30(2):175-79.

Jianguo Liu, Gretchen C. Daily, Paul R. Ehrlich and Gary W. Luck (2003), "Effects of Household Dynamics on Resource Consumption and Biodiversity", *Nature* 421, 530-33.

Krishnakumar, Asha (2003) "Understanding Dementia", *Frontline*, vol. 20, Issue 06, 15-28 March 2003.

Lazaroff, C. (2003) "Smaller Households Lead to Vanishing Biodiversity", *Environmental News Service*.

Lefort, R. (2010), "700 Children Born with Genetic Disabilities due to Cousin Marriages Every Year", *The Telegraph*, 22 August 2010.

McClintock, M.K., S. Bullivant, S. Jacob, N. Spencer, B. Zelano, C. Ober (2005), "Human Body Scents: Conscious Perceptions and Biological Effects", *Chem Senses*, January 2005; 30 Suppl 1:135-37.

Nautiyal, C.S., P.S. Chauhan, Y.L. Nene (2007), "Medicinal Smoke Reduces Airborne Bacteria", *J. Ethnopharmacology*, 114, 446-51.

Saxena, M., B. Sengupta, P. Pandya (2007a), "A Study of the Impact of Yagya on Indoor Microbial Environments", *Ind. J. Air Pollut. Control*, VII, 6-15.

Saxena, M., B. Sengupta, P. Pandya (2007b), "Comparative Studies of Yagya *vs* Non-Yagya in Microbial Environments", *Ind. J. Air Pollut. Control*, VII, 16-24.

Schmahl, G., K.A. Al-Rasheid, F. Abdel-Ghaffar, S. Klimpel, H. Mehlhorn (2010), "The Efficacy of Neem Seed Extracts (Tre-san, MiteStop on a Broad Spectrum of Pests and Parasites", *Parasitol Res.*, 107, 261-69.

Subapriya, R., S. Nagini (2005), "Medicinal Properties of Neem Leaves: A Review", *Curr Med Chem Anticancer Agents*, 5, 149-156.

13 - Symposium participants on a break

Contributors

Bhandari, C.M., M.Sc. (Physics) from I.I.T., Kanpur; A.I.F.C., Dehra Dun and M.A., National Defence College, New Delhi, joined the Indian Foreign Service in 1974 and after diplomatic assignments in Indian Missions in Bangkok, Oslo, Lagos and Canberra, served as India's Consul General in Toronto, Canada and Ambassador to Cambodia, United Arab Emirates, Poland and Lithuania. He has written three books: *Saving Angkor* (1996) on Cambodia's Indian Heritage; *Jouney to Heaven: Kailash Mansarovar* (1998) and *Yoga Shakti* (2002). All three books are currently out of print but revised edition of *Yoga Shakti* came in Jan 2010 and that of *Journey to Heaven* is expected shortly. He is an avid practitioner of Yoga and India's Vedic heritage but loves empowerment from every other culture and religion. He retired from Diplomatic career in June 2009 and now devotes full time to grassroots development in his native state of Uttarakhand [*address*: 416, Garhi Cantt., Dehra Dun - 248 003 (Uttarakhand), *e-mail*: <cmbhandari@gmail.com>].

Duvvuru, Jamuna, a Professor of Psychology, after obtaining her Ph.D. in Gero-Psychology, she continued her research in gerontology studying status and patterns of ageing among various special concern groups, cognitive ageing, elder care, longevous individuals, healthy ageing, intergenerational issues of elder care, etc. She underwent training in social gerontology at International Institute of Ageing, Malta, as UNFPA Fellow (1992); recipient of Sandoz Fellowship (1996-97) to undergo advanced training in ageing at Gerontology Center, Penn. State University; Visiting Scientist at TMIG Tokyo (1998) ; Fulbright Fellow to conduct research at Gerontology Center, Penn. State University and University of Southern California (2003-04); SICI Fellow at St. Thomas University,

Fredericton, Canada (2010). She has published a modest number of articles in the area of ageing and directed various research projects in the area of gerontology. She was the president of Association of Gerontology — India (AGI) during 2006-08 and vice president of Academy of Psychologists (AOP), India [*address*: Professor, Head and Coordinator, Centre for Research on Ageing, Department of Psychology, Sri Venkateswara University, Tirupati, *e-mail*: <agi2008tirupati @gmail.com>, <jxd172@gmail.com>].

Jhaveri, Madhusudan, PhD (Structural Engineering) and PE (Registered Professional Engineer, Massachusetts), has contributed to numerous presentations, poetry recitals, technical conferences, WAVES conferences, Newman Lectures and wrote a poetry book in Gujarati, numerous poems in Hindi and articles in various magazines. Dr Jhaveri was an invited panelist at the RUAH Panel to discuss on Spirituality and Work: Similarities and Differences. She chaired Annual National Convention of the Antarrashtriya Hindi Association held at Rochester (New York) in 1999; Sanskrit Bharati Teachers Convention of Maharastra held at Barashi (Maharashtra) in 2000/2001. Dr Jhaveri was the guest speaker on Gandhi and Ahiṁsā, at Sherbourne (Massachussetts). Dr Jhaveri also represented Hinduism at a two-day conference on Conversions and Conflict Resolutions held at George Mason University (2001) [*address*: Center for Indic Studies, and Department of Civil and Environmental Engineering, University of Massachusetts Dartmouth, 285 Old Westport Road, Dartmouth, MA 02747, USA, *e-mail*: <mjhaveri@umassd.edu>].

Khaitan, Mona, PhD in Hindu Studies, has contributed several articles on subjects such as Sva-Dharma, Vedic Values, Yoga, Karma Yoga, etc. in journals of international repute. She has also participated in conferences at international level such as World Association of Vedic Studies held at Houston, Texas, in 2006; Youth Conference 2006 on Hindu Values, Taunton, Massachusetts; The New England Conference of the Association for Asian Studies, University of Massachusetts, Dartmouth, Massachusetts, in 2006. Her book *Right Action: Key to Liberation and a Part of All Paths in the Bhagavad Gita* is in press [*address*: MassBay Community College, 50 Oakland St.,

Wellesley Hills, MA 02481, USA, *e-mail*: <mkhaitan@massbay.edu>].

Kalavar, (Josi) Jyotsna, Associate Professor of Human Development & Family Studies at Penn State University. Dr Kalvar's primary research interest is in the area of diverse experiences of ageing, including ageism, homebound seniors, immigrant seniors, intergenerational relationships, and seniors residing in long-term care institutions. As a Fulbright Research Scholar, Dr Kalavar spent her sabbatical year examining the experiences of seniors living in "pay-and-stay homes" in India. Dr Kalavar has completed or has ongoing projects with collaborators in New Zealand, United Kingdom, India, and Tanzania [*address*: Associate Professor, Penn State New Kensington, Human Development & Family Studies, 3550 Seventh Street Road, New Kensington, PA 15068 (USA), *e-mail*: <jmk18@psu.edu>]

Mishra, Rabi N., had his doctorate in Economics from University of Mumbai. While pursuing his Post Doctorate at the Economics Department of Harvard University, USA, he felt the urge to propagate the beauty of Indian culture by way of lectures at various places in USA. The current article is one of the "by-products" of that "urge." Dr Mishra works as a senior executive in the Indian financial sector. [*address*: A-17, Dhanastra, 122-N.P.Marg, Colaba, Mumbai-400005, *e-mail* : <rabi60@gmail.com> <rmishra@fas.harvard.edu>].

Misra, V.D., presently senior Professor, has been associated with the Dept. of Sociology, University of Lucknow, since 1971. He did his Masters in Ancient Indian History and Sociology with distinction and Doctorate in Sociology from the same University. His areas of research are: Indology, Sociology, Indian Culture, Religion, Philosophy, Childhood and Youth, Gender Development, Sports and Indian Diaspora. He is a member of several professional bodies and has produced 35 PhDs. He has written many books and several important articles in national and international journals [*address*: Department of Sociology, University of Lucknow, Lucknow (UP) *e-mail*: <misravd@hotmail.com>].

Patil, V.T., M.A., Ph.D., D.Litt., has occupied a number of important positions in academia in the last 40 years of teaching, research and academic administration: UGC National Fellow; Professor and Chairman, Department of Political Science, Karnataka University; Director, UGC Academic Staff College; Jawaharlal Nehru Professor of Political Science, Karnataka University; Vice-Chancellor, Pondicherry Central University; and Adjunct Professor, Centre for Indic Studies, University of Massachusetts, Dartmouth, USA. Prof. Patil has authored a substantial number of books and research papers and his work on Nehruvian and Gandhian Studies has received national and international recognition. Presently he is Emeritus Professor, The Global Open University, Nagaland, India [*address*: Flat No. 3, Devi Apartment, Yallakki Shettar Colony, Vidyagiri, Dharwad – 580 004, Karnataka, *e-mail*: <vtpatil14@ gmail.com>].

Satapathy, D.R., received his Ph.D. and D. Litt. in Philosophy, M.A. in Philosophy, M.A. in English Literature, B.A. Hons. in Sanskrit, has taught Philosophy and English Literature more than thirty five years. Has authored Five books, *Shankara's Conception of the World and Other Essays*, 1984 and *Doctrine of Maya in Advaita Vedanta*, (available in amazon.com) 1992.; *Studies in Vedantism: the Doctrines, Dialogues and Debates*, *The Concept of Person* and *A Treatise on Upanishads* are coming shortly. His focus is Western and Indian Philosophy, Tradition and Contemporary, the Comparative Philosophy, Culture and Religion, Hindu Religious Thought, Vedanta and Buddhist Studies, Indology, Sanskrit Studies; Vedic and Classical, The Shruti and Smrti and its Ethical Conceptions, Feminism. Nominated as American Man of the Year 1998, is placed among men and women of achievement of Asia and the World 1992, European and American Who's Who 1993 and 1995. Professor and Head of the PG Department of Philosophy and Religion, Ravenshaw University; Visiting Professor of Utkal University of Culture in the School of Language and Literature, engaged in higher research, produced and examiner of PhDs. with fifty papers, presentations, seminars, symposia, conferences, national and international, to his credit [*address*: Professor of Philosophy English Language and Literature Opposite P.H. Section:1, Water Works Road, PURI - 752 002 (Orissa), *e-mail*: <satapathyr@gmail.com>].

Satapathy, Gautam, is a PhD Fellow in Philosophy, Central University of Hyderabad, served as lecturer in philosophy Zakir Husain College as well as Deshbandhu College, University of Delhi. Taught as Visiting-teaching in Modern Philosophy, Phenomenology, Existentialism and Marxism in Ravenshaw College (University), Orissa. M A. Utkal (Philosophy), M. Phil. Central University of Hyderabad. Published in Kluwer Academic Publishers USA, the paper entitled 'Metaphysics, West and East, Bosanquet and Shankara,' also published in Indic Centre UMASS and SACP, USA. Invited to session chair in Notre Dame University Fall 2006 on 'Modernity.' Also invited to session chair in American Philosophical Association along with Prof. Shelley Wilcox, Temple University, USA. Associated with WAVES; USA and India, presented papers in several conferences and workshops of national and international importance like SIPR, SACP, IWPC, Japan World Congress on Aesthetics and Ethics, submitted papers on Buddhism and Modernity and Humanistic Buddhism to ISB Emory, USA, paper in Schopenhauer Society. Associated with academic exchanges and interactions with Wharton and Harvard Business Schools, USA, Catholic University Washington and Submitted papers in Central University of Hyderabad and Utkal University Seminars, AOPA ands IPC as around twenty papers and presentations he has to his credit [*address*: *Lecturer in Philosophy*, Zakir Husain College, University of Delhi, *e-mail*: <akshpd@gmail.com>].

Singh, Bal Ram, is the Director of Center for Indic Studies at UMass Dartmouth, where he teaches a course on Science of Kriyayoga. Dr Singh as a Professor of Biophysical Chemistry and Henry Dreyfus Teacher-Scholar at University of Massachusetts Dartmouth, and the Director of Botulinum Research Center, has been conducting research for 20 years at UMass Dartmouth on the molecular mode of action of botulinum and tetanus neurotoxins, and lately also on yoga, mind, and consciousness. Dr Singh has published about 175 research articles, has edited three books, including *India's Intellectual Traditions and Contributions to the World* (DKPW, 2010), and *Origin of Indian Civilization* (DKPW, 2010), and has obtained 3 patents. He has published over three dozen scholarly articles on issues related to Indian tradition, culture, and philosophy. He is Associate Editor of the International Journal of Indian Culture and Business Management. Dr Singh is President of BBTech, Inc., Dartmouth, MA, and Managing Director of BBTech Herbal in India. He is also Manager of a girl's school, Kuruom Vidyalaya, which he has established in his native village in India [*address*: Director, Center for Indic Studies, University of Massachusetts, Dartmouth, 285 Old Westport Road, Dartmouth, MA 02747 (USA); *e-mail*: <bsingh@umassd.edu>].

Tripathi, Divya, is a meritorious Sanskrit scholar. She did postgraduation and Ph.D. in Sanskrit and won Gold Medals for topping M.A. (Sanskrit) and M.A. (all subjects) from Panjab University, Chandigarh. She won many contests in debate and poetry recitation and was adjudged All India Second Best NCC Cadet. Dr Tripathi accomplished Post-Doctoral Research under UGC plan. She has presented papers in scores of national and international seminars. These presentations were also published in reputed research publications. During the last 28 years of her illustrious career as Associate Professor, she has been the member of Board of Studies and Indic Studies in Kurukshetra University. Dr Tripathi is Editor-in-chief of research journal *Coherence* published by DAV College, Yamunanagar (Haryana) [*address*: Head of the Department of Sanskrit, DAV College for Girls, Yamunanagar – 135 001, Haryana, *e-mail*: <divya16tripathi@ yahoo.co.in>].

Index